INDIA BOOKVARSITY

LOTUS CHOICES

Editor: Mahendra Kulasrestha

Classics Revived
for an
Ultramodern World

INTELLECT INDIA

Companion volume of
CULTURE INDIA

Containing details of the various aspects of the very rich intellectual history of India: The Vedas, Upanishads, Sutras, Buddhism, Jainism, Epics, Classics, Folklore and Technical Literature

4263/3, Ansari Road,
Darya Ganj, New Delhi-110002

INTELLECT INDIA

A.A. Macdonell

Emeritus Professor of
Sanskrit, Oxford
University

Source: *India's Past*, by
A.A. Macdonell,
Published by
Clarendon Press,
Oxford, 1927

INTELLECT INDIA
ISBN: 81-8382-124-3

Published by:
LOTUS PRESS
4263/3, Ansari Road,
Darya Ganj, New Delhi-110002
Ph.: 32903912, 23280047
E-mail: lotus_press@sify.com

Printed at: Anand Sons, Delhi

Editorspeak

Romancing with Ideas

India's intellect did not show much in Science, but it did glow in matters of philosophy, religion, languages, literature, arts, medicine, etc. It developed the unique concepts of Atman and Brahman, Karma and rebirth, Mukti or Nirvana, religion with as well as without God, many kinds of interrelated religions and philosophies—not one with a single book—one of which, Buddhism, spread without use of any kind of force in most parts of the then known world—and which is reviving once again in the much troubled modern times to solve the present-day problems of unprecedented, inhuman violence, dreaded terrorism, etc. The country's eclectic nature in these respects is the direct result of its all consuming, tolerant and essentially truth-oriented examination and search into Life—its greatest asset in matters of living and survival in difficult times—which now, perhaps, needs another powerful thrust, a radically new approach, in the so called ultra-modern times, to discover the mystery and purpose—if any there be—of human and all other life in the otherwise indifferent, passive, conscienceless cosmos—as well as the unbelievably poverty-stricken and callous world.

Every country has its characteristics, good, ordinary and bad, which the countrymen should know about, of their own as well as of the others, especially in the present times when, perhaps for the first time in history prosperity seems to be increasing, science progressing in a most unimaginable manner, and life being globalised as it had never done before. Each country has its own culture and is different in many respects from the others. There are many countries and cultures but only two—India and China—are living since their inception, others belong to middle ages, of which many have died. If a study of Violence in history is made, it would reflect that the cultures which attacked others did not survive, and those which did not attack are still breathing—India and China being prominent among them. This is somewhere related to their philosophies of life. And they are once again revving up to play their roles in the world. It is a good sign for us that Indian spiritualism, yoga, as also our many religions, are making an impact in the Western world and a new kind of life-style is emerging for the younger new generation. China could also have participated in this globalised living, had its bothside language problem not created walls; the Indian's facility with English and the relative simplicity of Hindi if one wants to learn it, is certainly an enormous plus for us and the Westerners to join hands in the growth of a new global civilisation.

The **India Bookvarsity** series of suitably edited quality works already produced by Western scholars many years ago is aimed at serving this purpose. This particular book is a companion volume of the earlier published *Culture India,* which presents a general overview of the various aspects of Indian culture, contributed by authorities in their respective fields. The present one provides material on just one aspect of its culture, by a celebrity scholar of the early twentieth century, Prof. A.A. Macdonell of Oxford University. His contribution to Indology is remarkable, and what I find so commendable in his work is his sympathetic yet objective approach to ancient Indian culture. His writing is simple and very easy to understand, and this is why I have chosen three-fourth of his famous work *India's Past: A Survey of Her Literatures, Religions, Languages and Antiquities,* for this volume. It contains the Vedas, Brahmanas, Aranyakas, Upanishads, Sutras, Buddhism, Jainism, Epics, Classics, Folklore and all kinds of Technical Literature, including the various philosophical systems, astronomy, medicine, etc. The picture he draws of all this material is quite enchanting, and just enough for the general intelligent reader. He himself calls it the 'Intellectual' history of India, and the work covers the main points only, though the material is 'so extensive'.

The discovery of the Sanskrit language and the ancient Indian culture in modern times was started in the nineteenth century by English and German scholars like Maxmuller, Bloomfield, Roth, Macdonell, etc., etc.—the names are in fact too many to note—and despite the harms of colonialism, it did open entirely unexpected new vistas of Indian culture which impressed the more educated and reasonable persons primarily in European countries and later on in America. It is ironic that Maxmuller was inspired and supported by the East India Company to publish the Sacred Books of the East in order to promote Christianity in India and other eastern countries, but the gigantic scholarly project—altogether

50 volumes were published which are still regarded as the most comprehensive and authentic—but it served the causes of Hinduism, Buddhism, etc., instead of doing even an iota of good to the religion of Jesus Christ. And Maxmuller himself changed his views drastically. The study of Sanskrit and the literature written in it 'originated in the Western world of scholarship several new sciences, Comparative Philology, Comparative Mythology, Comparative Religion and Comparative Literature', according to Macdonell as well as many others. It also influenced the study of history in the world in a most fundamental way.

This writer strongly feels that we as Indians are not aware of these significant factors of our national-cultural life. At a time when we are spreading in large numbers all over the world, in the West in particular, and most of us are fairly well educated in comparison to migrants of other countries, when many of our boys and girls themselves are keenly looking for their roots in an effort to build up their personalities and careers, such reading is a need of the times. This work provides in a nutshell Indian people's romance with the world of ideas and imagination, which in comparison to other countries, sounds quite different and dealing with the fundamental problems of human and other life in as many shapes as possible—which will hold their validity till other better and more convincing ideas present themselves to light up the dark main road of life and its alleys.

Authorspeak

India's Intellectual History

THIS work summarizes India's intellectual history, which in its various aspects has been the subject of my studies for slightly more than half a century (1875 to 1926). It sets forth the mental development of the most easterly branch of Aryan civilization since it entered India by land, till it came in contact by sea with the most westerly branch of the same civilization after a separation of at least 3,000 years.

The ground covered by the present volume is this. The introductory chapter describes the physical aspects of India and their resulting effect on migrations of population into this area. The next chapter tells of the language, the literature, and the religion of the earliest period of the Aryans in India. Then follows an account of the later Vedic period and the introduction of writing. The fourth chapter describes the early post-Vedic age, including the rise of Jainism and Buddhism as well as their art. The next chapter deals with the epic and classical literature of India. The sixth chapter is concerned with Indian stories, fairy tales, and fables, together with their important place in world literature. The seventh chapter treats of the various aspects of technical literature such as grammar, lexicography, law, practical arts, medicine, astronomy, and mathematics.

The range of our knowledge of India's past is now so extensive that the information supplied by this book could only cover the main and essential points. Its contents are meant, within a small compass, to direct both the English and the Indian reader through the long tract of time from the beginning of the Vedic age down to the epoch when the modern European became acquainted with the Indo-Aryan. These two civilizations, starting from a common source, have after a separation of at least 3,000 years, again become united during the last four centuries, representing together a quarter of the total of the earth's inhabitants. All this, as set forth in the following pages, will, I trust, contribute something to clearer mutual understanding by two civilizations which in their origin were one and the same.

1927, Oxford. *—A.A. Macdonell*

Contents

1.

The Diamond-shaped Country

A GLANCE at the physical map of the world suffices to show that no country forming part of the old continents, in which the civilization of mankind has been evolved, is so isolated by nature as India. Rhomboidal in outline or roughly diamond-shaped, it extends from its northern angle in Kashmir to Cape Comorin as its southernmost extremity; and from the mouths of the Indus in the west to somewhat beyond the estuary of the Brahmaputra in the east, its utmost length, some 1,900 miles, being about equal to its greatest breadth. Its total area, which, excluding Burma (Myanmar), covers a surface of rather more than one million and a half square miles, is somewhat larger than fifteen times that of Great Britain.

It is divided by the tropic of Cancer (23° N. lat.) into a northern and a southern triangle. These are separated from west to east across the greater width of the peninsula by the Vindhya and other connected ranges that lie between the longitude of Mount Abu (73° E.) and Parasnath Hill (87° E.). The northern triangle consists of an alluvial plain, which in an earlier geological age formed the floor of the ocean, but in later, though still prehistoric times, became raised above the level of the sea. It is continental in character, being surrounded by mountain ranges on all sides.

On the west it is shut off from the neighbouring countries of Asia by high mountains. On the east it is separated from Burma by a series of high hills and by impenetrable jungle. On the north it is bounded by the most stupendous range in the world, at least 1,400 miles in length and about 19,000 ft. in height, its peaks varying from 25,000 to 29,000 ft. In this great barrier there are some mountain tracks by which men have found their way to India. Such are the passes from the Pamirs by Gilgit, as well as those from Tibet by Leh, by the gorge of the Sutlej, and by Sikkim.

But these are not highways by which migrations or invasions from the north have reached or could reach southwards to India. Nor has the eastern frontier, protected by hills and jungles, ever been exposed to hostile attack. It is only on the western side, though even this is guarded by almost continuous ranges of lofty hills, that from time immemorial immigration, conquest, and commerce made their way before 1500 A.D. by narrow roads into India. Access can here be gained either from southern Balochistan by the rocky track leading to the Indus delta, or from Afghanistan by the Bolan, the Tochi, and the Khaibar passes, as well as by the river valleys of the Gomal, the Kurram, and the Kabul, to the banks of the Indus farther north.

Only through the western gateways have passed the two great invasions that have vitally affected the fortunes of India. By this way came in prehistoric times the wave of Aryan migration that overspread India with its civilization from that day to this. It was perhaps two thousand years or more afterwards that the Semitic conquest by Islam began on the western frontier, about 700 A.D. A considerable part of India was held under this alien despotic sway for more than seven hundred years, down to the middle of the eighteenth century. This dominion, though unifying India politically, did not essentially modify its civilization, in spite of the fact that one-fifth of the entire population professes Islam at the present day. With the exception of the Greeks, from 326 B.C. till about 200 A.D., only Asiatics have come in contact with the continental half of India by land.

This great northern plain is enclosed not only by mountain ranges but by rivers on every side. Two of the three largest of these rise close together in Tibet, near the great Kailasa group of peaks and the Manasarowar lake at the back and about the middle of the Himalayan barrier. The Indus in the first half of its course follows a north-westerly direction; then, bending round the extremity of the Himalayan chain, it flows southward till it falls into the Arabian Sea just north of the tropic of Cancer. Its whole course is about 1,500 miles in length. The Brahmaputra, rising slightly to the east of Lake Manasarowar (*c.* 83° E.), after an easterly course of many hundreds of miles through Tibet, urns southward at the end of the Himalayan range (*c.*96° E.), and, flowing slightly westward of Dacca, finally enters the Bay of Bengal somewhat to the south of the tropic of Cancer, almost opposite the mouths of the Indus on the other side of India. Its whole length is about 1,800 miles.

The third great river of northern India, the Ganges (in Sanskrit Ganga), which is about 1,540 miles long, rises (*c.* 80° E.) somewhat to the south-west of the sources of the Indus and the Brahmaputra. Breaking through the southern range of the central Himalaya, it flows in a south-easterly direction through the eastern half of the alluvial plain of Hindustan. At Goalando it joins the Meghna, the largest and most easterly estuary of the Brahmaputra. Between this and the Hughi, the most westerly and main branch of the Ganges, lies the combined delta of the two mighty rivers.

Parallel to the southern slopes of the Vindhya range, which shuts off the northern plain, flows the Narmada river from its source at Amarkantak (82° E.) with a slight northerly trend past Jabalpur (80°E.) and then westward, by Bharuch (thirty miles from its mouth) to the Bay of Kutch.

The area of the great alluvial plain of northern India is called by the Persian name of Hindustan, the 'country of the Indus', the river on the western side of the country, with which foreigners first became acquainted.

The area of the great alluvial plain of Hindustan is shut off by the Vindhya range, which forms the northern buttress of the Deccan, the name of southern India, the whole of which lies within the tropics south of the Narmada river. It is a rocky plateau, bounded on both sides by high ridges of hills called Ghats, which are separated by narrow strips of lowland on the west from the Arabian Sea, and on the east from the Bay of Bengal. The plateau slopes gradually from the western Ghats, which average about 3,000 ft. in height, to the eastern Ghats, which are 1,500 ft. high. Owing to this fact many of the rivers of the Deccan rise near its western edge and all fall into the eastern sea.

Though less exposed to migration and conquest from the rest of Asia than Hindustan, the Deccan did not oppose a difficult barrier to Aryan incursion within India itself, as is proved by the occurrence of Indo-Aryan inscriptions quite in the south, dating from as early as the third century B.C. But at a later period Muhammadan rule did not acquire so firm a hold of the Deccan as it did of north Hindustan.

Contact with the outer world by land has always been restricted to north Hindustan. More than 500 years before Christ the region on both sides of the Indus, comprising the western Punjab and Sindh, from the district in ancient times called Gandhara (with its capital Taxila, twenty miles north of Rawalpindi) to the mouths of the Indus, became (from 530 B.C.) and remained part of the neighbouring Persian Empire till the destruction of that empire by Alexander in 331 B.C.

After that conqueror's brief invasion of the Punjab in 326 B.C., and his death at Babylon in 323 B.C., his Graeco-Bactrian successors remained in touch with the north-west till the second century A.D. There followed some minor invasions in this region, but no permanent conquest was established till the foundation of the Muhammadan Empire, about 1200 A.D.

The Deccan was really more completely isolated from the rest of the world by the sea than north Hindustan by its mountain barriers, till little five centuries ago. While every cape and bay of the Mediterranean and East Africa were known to the Phoenicians, the coasts of India seem to have remained unknown to them. But the evidence available warrants the belief that maritime commerce between India and Babylon by the Persian Gulf nourished from about 700 to 480 B.C. Specially Indian products—

rice, peacocks, and sandalwood—were known in the west by their Tamil designations. That they must have been imported from the west coast of India into Babylon by sea is an inference to be drawn from an early Buddhist book, dating from perhaps 400 B.C.

The Indian products must have been first imported not later than the sixth century B.C., because direct intercourse between Babylon and India practically ceased after 480 B.C., and because rice and peacocks must have reached Greece at the latest by about 460 B.C., so as to become familiar at Athens in the time of Sophocles (495-406 B.C.). Corroboration of the date of the early trade between Mesopotamia and India is supplied by the alphabetical Phoenician writing, which was introduced into India and must have been in use there not later than about 700 B.C. A similar conclusion is indicated by numismatic evidence: the oblong silver coins bearing no legend and known as *puranas,* which are the oldest coinage of India and are represented on Buddhist bas-reliefs of the second century B.C., resemble the coins of Babylon of about 500 B.C. and are not improbably an imitation of them.

When Babylon and Egypt declined, the merchants of Yemen in South Arabia entered into the commercial inheritance of those two countries, and the greater part of the trade with India, as well as with equatorial Africa, passed into their hands. But the Arabs do not seem to have been among the early sea-going races, though southern Arabian tribes were from remote ages the carriers of the East. Their caravans traversed the Arabian peninsula in every direction, but their traffic was by land and not by sea.

With the establishment of Islam, in 622 A.D., the

trade of the Arabs spread not only on land over a great part of Asia Minor, the Black Sea region, northern Africa and southwestern Europe, but also acquired control of the harbours of the Arabian Sea and the African coasts, as well as of the maritime route from the Persian Gulf to India and China.

Contact with the rest of Asia by sea thus remained restricted to the coasting trade on the western side of India down to the end of the fifteenth century A.D. Then for the first time India became known to the nations of Europe by maritime intercourse. The discovery of the ocean route to India by Vasco da Gama, in 1498, brought India not only within the range of world commerce, but under the influence of Western civilization. It led to the establishment of a new empire which, though like that of Rome in being incorporated and ruled from the centre, was gradually trained to progress and the attainment of autonomous powers. The result is that India became more westernized than any other Asiatic country.

In the new era the European settlers, whose chief interest was commercial, became acquainted, though in a very imperfect manner, with the latest forms of Indian language, custom, and religion. But after the consolidation of British rule, in the middle of the eighteenth century, administrators and scholars began to study with increasing intensity India's past in all its aspects—literary, linguistic, religious, archaeological. The result of their aggregate researches is that the history of Indian civilization has in every direction been reconstructed and revealed to the modern world. It can now be presented to the reader as a whole, not only as a picture of the past, but as a guide for the days to come.

After Alexander's invasion, in 326 B.C., we have from about 300 B.C. fairly clear archaeological evidence of man's activities in India. This supplies the basis on which the early political history of India has been established. But before the third century B.C. we have only glimmerings of what happened on Indian soil. We have had nothing more than prehistoric graves in the south and some cyclopean walls at Rajagriha in the north to throw uncertain light on the remoter past. Suddenly there has been revealed by the operations of the archaeological survey of India, a new class of objects which may illuminate much better the prehistoric period of the country. At present (1926), however, they furnish insufficient evidence to establish their age and origin.

These finds lie at two sites in the Indus region, 400 miles apart, at Harappa in the lower Punjab, about half-way between Multan and Lahore on the railway, and at Mohenjo-daro in the Larkana district of Sindh on the Indus. At both sites there are numerous artificial mounds rising as much as sixty feet above the plain, and especially conspicuous along dried-up beds of the main stream of the Indus. There is little doubt that this region will prove a valuable area for systematic archaeological exploration.

At Mohenjo-daro has been found in the dry bed of the river a Buddhist *stupa* of the second century A.D. Below this have been excavated at least two other strata containing brick structures, the character and age of which can only be conjectured. The remains at these two sites consist of pottery, painted and plain, some hand-made, some turned on the wheel; terracottas; new types of coins; dice and chessmen; a number of engraved and inscribed seals. The legends on the stone seals are engraved in an unknown script, the figures and style being different from anything in Indian art; but they show a certain general affinity to the pictographs of the Mycenaean age. The coins here found may turn out to be the oldest in existence, the earliest as yet known being the Lydian coins of the seventh century B.C. Iron is found only in the latest layer of these deposits. The culture here revealed must have extended over many centuries, but seems to have come to an end not long before the rise of the Maurya dynasty (320 B.C.).

Nothing very definite can be said about this forgotten civilization. It may have developed in the Indus valley and have died out without any influence on the civilization of India proper. Similarity has already been discovered between plaques found here and tablets found at Susa. This similarity may point to intercourse between Susa and north-western India. It is possible that the people who made these seals were in close contact with Sumerian civilization, and borrowed their artistic style and the elements of their writing from the Sumerians at some period about 3000-2800 B.C. Nothing about them was known in England till the appearance of some articles and letters regarding them by Sir John Marshall and others in the last quarter of 1924.

2.

The Vedas

We are able to infer safely from the evidence of the earliest phase of Indian literature that in remote prehistoric times certain warlike tribes invaded India from the north-west, and, gradually spreading first to the east and then to the south, subjected the aborigines and imposed both their speech and their civilization on almost the entire country. The approximate date of this invasion remains conjectural, but there are good grounds for regarding the fourteenth century B.C. as not improbable.

The language spoken by the conquerors was the earliest form of Sanskrit preserved in the hymns that the poet-priests of the invaders began to compose after they had entered the country. It was not known that this language is closely allied to Persian, Greek, Latin, Teutonic, Celtic, and Slavonic.

Their relationship is illustrated by such words as Sanskrit *matar,* Greek μητηρ, Latin *mater,* Old Irish *mathir,* English *mother;* Skt. *sunu,* Lithuanian *sunu,* Old High German *sunu,* English *son*. Known at an earlier stage than any of the others, the ancient Indian branch has been of prime importance in the history of philology. The evidence indicating the region where the invading

Aryans entered India consists mainly of geographical data to be found in the early hymns. From the names of the rivers there mentioned it may safely be concluded that the area occupied by the newcomers lay between the Indus and the Sutlej, bounded on the north by the Himalaya, with a fringe of settlements to the east and west of these limits. This evidence is corroborated by that of the fauna and flora referred to in the earliest period. The lion, to whose habits western India is well adapted, is familiar, but the tiger is never mentioned. Rice, the natural habitat of which is in the south-east, is unknown.

The ancient Aryan language has been minutely examined, and the historical evidence contained in its literature extracted. The final result has been that the two sources have taken an important place both in the history of Indian civilization and in the foundation and development of four branches of Western study. For they are respectively the basis not only of nearly all the vernaculars and of the indigenous religions of modern India, but have also originated in the Western world of scholarship several new sciences, Comparative Philology, Comparative Mythology, Comparative Religion, and Comparative Literature, which between them have made a large contribution to the culture and enlightenment of the world.

The oldest book of the ancient period is, for various reasons, the most important work of Indian literature. It is the earliest product not only of Indian, but of Indo-European literature. It is therefore capable of shedding light in various directions on prehistoric phases of language (such as inflexion, accent, and metre), of religion, and of civilization in general. Many of these problems would be insoluble without its evidence. The investigation of its religion led in the second half of the 19th century to the foundation of the sciences of Comparative Mythology and Comparative Religion. The Indian religion of Buddhism could not be fully understood by one not knowing this Veda, for its relation to the latter is like that of the New Testament to the Old. Finally, it has been the authoritative sacred book, for over 3,000 years, of myriads of Hindus: prayers derived from it are uttered by them even at the present day.

The word 'Veda', primarily meaning 'knowledge (from *vid,* 'to know'), virtually signifies 'sacred knowledge or scripture', and expresses the whole character of the ancient period of Indian literature, which bears an exclusively religious stamp: even the latest productions of that age, though not directly religious, were ancillary to Vedic religion. In the Vedic period three literary strata can be clearly distinguished: the first is that of the four Vedas, which consist of hymns, prayers, and spells addressed to the gods; the second, that of the Brahmanas or ritual treatises; the third, that of the Upanishads or theosophical works, the basis of much of the later Indian philosophy.

The Four Vedas

The most ancient of the four Vedas is the *Rigveda,* 'The Veda of Verses' (*ric*), which consists chiefly of lyrics in praise of various gods. It may be called the 'book of psalms' as describing its contents most characteristically. From this Veda the other three largely borrow their subject-matter. The *Samaveda* has no independent importance, for it consists almost entirely of stanzas taken from the *Rigveda* for the ritual of the Soma sacrifice. The verses of the *Yajurveda* are for the most part also derived from the *Rigveda;* but about half of its contents, consisting of prose formulas, are original. Its subject-matter being arranged in the order in which it is employed in various sacrificial rites, it is characteristically the 'Veda of sacrificial spells (*yajus*)'.

For a considerable time these three Vedas alone were recognized as canonical scriptures, being in the next literary phase described as the 'threefold knowledge' (*trayi vidya,* Pali *tevijja*). The *Atharvaveda* came to be recognized as canonical only a good deal later than the other three; it is similar in form to the *Rigveda,* from which many of its hymns are taken; but the evidence both of its language and of its matter show that it was formed into a collection subsequently to the *Rigveda.* In spirit also it differs entirely from that Veda. For it does not deal with the higher gods, but for the most part with the demon world, being concerned with primitive ideas of witchcraft. It may appropriately be called the 'book of magical spells'.

As these two, the *Atharvaveda* and the *Rigveda,* record an earlier phase than any other sacred literature, they are of very high value to the student of the evolution of religious ideas. The arrangement of the *Rigveda,* unlike that of the *Sama-* and the *Yajur-veda,* was an historical one, for the intention of its ancient editors was simply to preserve this heritage of the past from change and destruction. The 1,028 hymns contained in it are grouped in ten books called *mandalas,* or cycles of varying length, except that the tenth embraces the same number as the first. Six of these books (II-VII) are homogenous, inasmuch as they are the work of the descendants of different Rishis, or seers. The hymns in these books all follow a uniform arrangement differing from that of the rest. They probably formed the nucleus to which the others were successively added.

It seems likely that the earliest addition to the 'family' books was the second part of Book I (51-191), because it resembles the 'family' books in its internal arrangement. The eighth book has a character of its own, and the first part of Book I (1-50) resembles it in some ways: it is therefore probable that these two formed the next addition. Book IX is of a peculiar type, as consisting entirely of Soma hymns, though these were evidently composed by authors of the same families as the hymns of Books II-VII, as appears from their having the same characteristic refrains.

It evidently did not come into being as a collection till after the first eight books had already been combined into a whole. For it was clearly formed into a homogeneous group of hymns addressed to the same deity by extracting all the Soma hymns from the eight books (which retain altogether only three) and then placing this uniform combination at the end of Book VIII. Though the Soma hymns in a collected form are thus comparatively late, there is good reason to believe that the composition of the individual Soma hymns as a whole belongs to an early part of the Vedic period, because it deals with a ritual going back to Indo-Iranian times.

The hymns of the tenth book clearly date from a later period than those of the first nine, because their composers were evidently familiar with the latter. That it is a collection of supplementary hymns is indicated by their being made up to the number (191) of those in the first book. It bears the general stamp of lateness, of which there is internal evidence of various kinds. The subject-matter, the mythology, and the language all show signs of a later age.

The passages taken from the *Rigveda* that appear in the other Vedas furnish evidence akin to various readings. They indicate that the text of the *Rigveda* is more original than the text of the others and that it has been handed down, with a remarkably high standard of integrity, from a time hardly later than 1000 B.C. There is good reason to believe that in the period lapsing between the composition of the hymns of the *Rigveda* and the constitution, by grammatical editors, of the extant phonetic text called *Samhita,* a very high level of verbal authenticity was maintained, though some unmistakable corruptions in detail can be detected. The most minute irregularities in the way of accent or alternate forms, which might have been removed with the utmost ease, have been retained unmodified.

Hence it may be said that in the Samhita text the actual words used by the ancient seers remain the same: thus *sumna* would not be substituted for *dyumna;* the changes would only apply to the phonetic forms required by the rules prevailing in the later phase of the Sanskrit language at the time when the sacred text was edited. Thus the old form of the words *tuam hi agne* would appear as *tvam hy agne,* 'for thou, O Agni'. But such modernization is only partial and not consistently applied. These modern phonetic changes are often in conflict with the metre; if read in accordance with the metre the actual words in the form used by the ancient seers would be restored except when there are corruptions due to mistakes of tradition in the earlier period, or to errors arising from grammatical theories in the later.

The statements of the Brahmanas justify the conclusion that the Samhita text was not constituted till after those treatises were completed, but the somewhat later manuals called Aranyakas and Upanishads contain evidence that the Samhita text of the *Rigveda* came into being before the post-Vedic ancillary literature concerned with Vedic grammar, phonetics, and other subjects arose, that is, about 600 B.C.

Preserving the Texts

Soon after the constitution of the Samhita text various means were devised to preserve that text intact. These devices have secured a faithfulness of tradition unparalleled in any other ancient literature. The first measure of this kind was the formation of a new text in which the Samhita is analysed in such a way as to restore every single word to its independent phonetically unmodified form, and to separate compounds into their elements. Thus *tvam hy agne* here appears as *tvam* | *hi* | *agne* |; and the compound *usarbudh* as *usah bhut*. This text, which is of a grammatically analytical character, is called the *Padapatha* or 'word-text'. Though it seems to have been composed soon after the Samhita text, it yet contains some analyses that are certainly erroneous.

Another measure for guarding the text of the *Rigveda* with still greater safety was the *Krama-patha* or 'step-text': here every word of the *Padapatha* occurs twice, being pronounced both after the preceding and before the following one. Thus *a b c d,* as representing the first four words, would be read as *ab, bc, cd.* There are some still more complex texts of this type, the sole purpose of which was to preserve the sacred book from loss or change. The phonetic treatises called *Pratisakhyas* were also of the nature of safeguards, as they set forth, with examples, the euphonic modifications necessary for turning the Pada into the Samhita text.

Lastly, a class of supplementary works called *Anukramanis*, or, 'Indexes', was compiled for the purpose of safeguarding the *Rigveda,* stating the number of the hymns, verses, words, and even syllables contained in the sacred text.

The four Vedas and three works of the Brahmana period have been preserved in an accented form. Owing to the necessity of reciting the sacred texts with absolute correctness, the marking of the accent was of great importance. The Vedic accent was a musical one, dependent on the pitch of the voice, like the ancient Greek accent; and it retained this character till long after the time of the grammarian Panini. But as the Greek, so the Vedic accent was, some time after the beginning of our era, transformed into a stress accent. While, however, in Greek the new stress accent remained on the same syllable as bore the old musical accent, the modern Sanskrit accent has no connexion with the ancient Vedic one, but depends on the quantity of the last two or three syllables, as in Latin. Thus the last syllable but one, if long, is stressed, e.g., *Kalidasa;* or the third from the end, if long, and followed by a short syllable, e.g., *brahmana* or *himalaya* ('abode of snow'). This change was brought about by the influence of Prakrit, or vernacular language, in which the stress can be traced to a time long antecedent to our era.

The most important Vedic accent is the *ud-atta* ('raised') equivalent to the Greek acute. The evidence of comparative philology proves that in the Vedic language the same syllable of a particular word bears it as that syllable did in proto-Aryan. For it is in the same place as in cognate Greek words, except where a new restrictive law of accentuation interferes, as in *hepta,* which is identical with the Vedic *sapta,* 'seven'; but *pheromenos,* Skt. *bharamanah.*

The Hymns and their Metre

The hymns of the *Rigveda* are composed in stanzas, generally of four lines, each hymn on the average containing about ten. The number of metres is fifteen, but three are by far the commonest, as four-fifths of the total number of stanzas are composed in them. The metrical unit is not, as in Greek, the foot (of two or three syllables), but the line, which by a curious coincidence is also called 'foot' (*pada*). The rhythm of the Vedic line is more elastic than that of Classical Sanskrit, for in the former the rhythm of only the last four or five syllables, while in the latter the whole line, is metrically regulated, except in one metre.

The main metrical principle in the Veda is the number of syllables in the line. In Indo-Iranian prosody this must have been the sole principle; for the *Avesta,* which forms stanzas containing lines of eight or eleven syllables, ignores quantity altogether. In Sanskrit, on the other hand, the quantity of each syllable was fixed in every metre except the loose octosyllabic iambic line of the epic stanza called *sloka.* Thus the metrical regulation of the line beginning with its last syllables first appeared in the Vedic period, and extended in Classical Sanskrit to every syllable. The rhythmical end of the Vedic line is called *vrtta,* 'turn', which corresponds etymologically to the Latin *versus.*

The metre is a valuable aid in restoring the original

form of the line, because the phonetic combination of later times applied between the finals and initials of contiguous words in the Samhita text reduces the number of syllables in the metrical line.

The commonest metre but one in the *Rigveda*, though it entirely disappeared in later Sanskrit, is the *gayatri*, which consists of three octosyllabic lines ending in two iambics, and forms one-fourth of all the stanzas in the *Rigveda*, e.g.:

sa nah piteva sunave,
Agne, supayano bhava;
sacasva nah suastaye.

To us, as father to his son,
O Agni, be accessible:
Do thou abide with us for weal.

The *tristubh* stanza is the commonest, two-fifths of the *Rigveda* being composed in this metre. It consists of four lines of eleven syllables ending trochaically. The following is an example:

Visnor nu kam viriani pra vocam
yah parthivani vimame rajamsi
yo askabhayad uttaram sadhastham,
vicakramanas trayadhorugayah.

I'll now proclaim the heroic powers of Vishnu,
Of him who measured out the earthly spaces,
Who has made firm the upper gathering station;
Who triply has stepped out, the widely striding.

The *jagati* stanza consists of four lines in which the final rhythm of the *tristubh* is increased by one syllable. This produces an iambic cadence:

Vi vrksan hanti uta hanti raksaso:
visvam bibhaya bhuvanam mahavadhat.
utanaga isate vrsniavato,
yat Parjanyah stanayan hanti duskrtah.

The trees he shatters and he strikes the demons down;
The whole world quakes in terror of his mighty strokes.
The very sinless man before the strong one flees,
When thundering Parjanya smites the miscreants.

Sayana Commentary

When European scholars first became acquainted with the *Rigveda,* they knew only the language and literature of Classical Sanskrit. They were thus confronted with the difficulty of interpreting poetry which dated from the remotest period of Indian civilization, which was composed in an ancient and isolated dialect, and which represented a world very different from the world known to them. Fortunately there existed a voluminous Sanskrit commentary to the *Rigveda* which explains every word of its hymns and which was written in the fourteenth century by a learned Vedic scholar named Sayana.

As the latter continually refers to ancient authorities, all that was considered necessary about 1850 was to translate the *Rigveda* according to his interpretations. But Roth, the founder of Vedic philology, pointed out that Sayana often gives several inconsistent explanations of a word in his comment on a single passage, as well as of the same word occurring in different passages. Even the interpretations of the numerous predecessors whom Yaska, the earliest Vedic commentator (c. 500 B.C.), mentions are often conflicting. One of them even asserted that the science of Vedic exposition was useless, the Vedic hymns being obscure, unmeaning, or mutually contradictory. Roth, in fact, declared that there was no continuity of interpretation going back to the time of the poets themselves, because interpretation could only arise when the meaning of the hymns had become uncertain. The commentators, he said, only preserved attempts at solving difficulties, and indeed betrayed a tendency to misinterpret both the language, and ideas of a bygone age by the scholastic notions prevailing in their own.

Roth consequently rejected the commentators as our chief guides in the interpretation of the Veda, holding that in its more obscure passages it must be self-interpreting. He accordingly proceeded to subject the *Rigveda* to an historical treatment within the range of Sanskrit, by carefully comparing all passages parallel in form and matter, and by paying special regard to context, grammar, and etymology, as well as consulting, though perhaps insufficiently, traditional interpretations. He also availed himself of the help supplied not only by the *Avesta,* which has such close affinities with the *Rigveda* in language and matter, but also by comparative philology, aids unknown to the traditional Indian scholar. The results of his labours are laid down in the great St. Petersburg Sanskrit Dictionary. Vedic scholars now all follow Roth's methods in the scientific investigation of the *Rigveda.* But they exploit more fully ths aid supplied by native traditional scholarship.

By close adherence to the critical method and by admitting all available evidence, many of the obscurities and difficulties still confronting the interpreter will, there is good reason to hope, ultimately vanish. In the generation that has passed since Roth's labours came to an end, many works and investigations have been published, such as books on anthropology and comparative religion, articles on grammar, metre, textual criticism, ritual, which when worked up as a whole, will contribute to decide numerous points of detail that are at present still obscure. A work like Prof. Bloomfield's *Rigveda Repetitions,* which enumerates something like 5,000 lines that recur in the *Rigveda*, will without doubt greatly advance the precision of translation, because hitherto the rendering of repeated passages has varied greatly owing to the translator overlooking the fact that he has been dealing with a repetition. There are other points in which this book will supply aid in the work of interpretation. Considering the accumulation of exegetical material during the last many years, the time seems to have arrived for summing up these results in a new translation of the *Rigveda.*

Religion of the Vedas

It may be said that the religion embodied in the *Rigveda* is a more important subject of study for the investigator of the history of religion than the religion of any other ancient sacred book; for **here we see the development of mythology and religion from the most primitive to an advanced stage, and gods coming into being before our very eyes: a transition being evolved from the animistic to the polytheistic stage,** from that in which natural phenomena are thought to be possessed of a soul like living beings to one in which they are personified, deified, and anthropomorphized as a polytheistic group, which is finally unified in a pantheistic sense.

We see deification here in all its phases, from the

beginning to the end of the scale. Thus the sky has only just begun to be touched by personification. In others it is more advanced, as in the case of Surya, the Sun, or Agni, Fire, who are much more anthropomorphic: their rays or flames, for instance, are called hands or tongues, though the poet can hardly imagine them apart from the actual phenomena of the solar orb or the actual element whose names they bear.

Others, like Indra, as an inheritance from a pre-Vedic period, are completely anthropomorphized, and can only conjecturally be identified with the phenomena that formed their starting-point. In later hymns we. find some quite abstract figures showing no traces of connexion with concrete phenomena, such as Prajapati, 'Lord of Creatures', or personifications of pure abstractions, such as Sraddha, 'Faith'. Finally, there appears in the last book of the *Rigveda* a tendency to arrive at the conception of a deity embracing all the gods as well as nature, that is, a single world-soul, though this is a conception not to be found fully developed till the period of the Upanishads.

The religion of the *Rigveda,* then, is a polytheistic one, concerned with the worship of gods, the great majority of whom are personifications of phenomena or powers of nature. The hymns are mainly invocations of these gods, meant to accompany the oblation of Soma juice and the offering of melted butter in the sacrificial fire. Many of the hymns no doubt originally arose independently of the sacrificial ritual and some of them came only secondarily to be applied to it. The number of the gods is stated in the *Rigveda* to be thirty-three, though there are a few groups that obviously cannot be included, in this total.

Only about twenty are, however, frequently invoked. The best known of them are the following: Dyaus and Varuna, gods of the sky; Surya, Mitra, Savitar, Pushan, Vishnu, solar divinities; the Asvins (the two horsemen) and Ushas (Dawn), deities of the morning; Indra, Apamnapat, Rudra, Maruts (Storm-gods), Vayu (Wind), Parjanya (Rain), Apas (Waters), gods of the air; Prithivi (Earth), Agni (Fire), Soma (draught of immortality), terrestrial deities; and Sindhu (Indus), Vipas (Beas), Sutudri (Sutlej), Sarasvati, Rivers of the Punjab.

When fully personified the gods are conceived as human in form; but their bodily parts are still often merely figurative terms: thus the arms of the Sun are nothing more than his rays; and the tongue and limbs of Agni are simply his flames. Some of the gods, especially Indra and the Maruts, appear as warriors; others are described as priests, as Agni and Brihaspati. All of them drive in celestial cars, drawn as a rule by two horses. Their food is the same as the favourite food of men: milk, butter, grain, and the flesh of sheep, goats, and cattle. This food is offered to them in the sacrifice, which is conveyed to them in heaven by the god of Fire, or which they come down in their cars to enjoy on the sacrificial ground. Their drink is the exhilarating Soma juice, cheered by draughts of which they live a life of bliss in heaven.

Gods for Power

The most prominent characteristic of the gods is power: they regulate the order of nature and vanquish the agencies of evil; they hold sway over all creatures; their laws cannot be thwarted; and they alone can fulfil desires. Another trait is their benevolence, for they bestow good gifts on men. They are also true and not deceitful, protecting the righteous and punishing the guilty. As the gods are nearly always conceived in connexion with the natural phenomena which they represent, their anthropomorphism is hardly ever complete, and each deity has few distinctive attributes, while many general divine qualities, such as power, brilliance, beneficence, and wisdom, are common to them all. They are therefore indefinite in outline, and may easily be identified one with another. Thus a poet addressing the Fire-god exclaims: 'Thou at thy birth, O Agni, art Varuna; when kindled thou becomest Mitra; in thee, O son of might, all gods are centred; thou art Indra to the worshipper.'

In later hymns the idea is even expressed that various gods are only different forms of a single divinity. Thus we find the verse: 'The one being priests speak of in many ways; they call it Agni, Yama, Matarisvan'(I. 64); and another: 'Priests and poets make into many the bird (i.e. the sun) which is but one' (X, 114). This idea, however, never ended in monotheism. In other late hymns the deities Aditi and Prajapati are identified not only with all the gods, but with nature as well. This germ of pantheism developed in the later Vedic literature of the Upanishads till it reached its final form in the Vedanta philosophy, which has remained the most popular system of the Hindus down to the present day.

The gods are regarded as immortal, but not as originally having been so. Their physical aspect is human, for face, arms, hands, fingers, and other anthropomorphic parts are attributed to them. But their shapes are shadowy. Thus of Vayu, Wind, it is said: 'His sound is heard, but his form is never seen.' Hence it is easy to understand that the ***Rigveda*** **contains no mention of images of the gods, still less of temples, which imply**

images. No reference to idols is to be found in the literature till two or three centuries before our era, in the Sutra period, and divine figures begin to appear in Buddhist sculptures from the second century B.C. onwards.

Goddesses play an insignificant role in the *Rigveda:* the only one to whom more than one or two hymns are addressed is Ushas, Dawn. She is, in fact, the only important goddess, for she is celebrated in about twenty hymns, which are the most beautiful in the *Rigveda.* Though Ushas, unlike most other divinities, receives no share of the Soma offering, the thoughts of the Vedic poets love to dwell on the beauties of the dawn, sometimes with a touch of sadness suggested by the eternally recurring phenomena of early morning in contrast with the fleeting nature of human life. The following translation, in which the *tristubh* metre of the original is imitated, may perhaps reflect some of the beautiful imagery occurring in these ancient hymns.

This light has come, of all the lights the fairest;
This brilliant brightness has been born, far-shining;
Urged onward for god Savitar's uprising,
Night now has yielded up her place to morning.

The sisters' pathway is the same, unending;
Taught by the gods, alternately they tread it.
Fair-shaped, of form diverse, yet single-minded,
Morning and night clash not, nor do they tarry.

Now Heaven's Daughter has appeared before us,
A maiden shining in resplendent garments.
Thou souran lady of all earthly treasure,
Auspicious Dawn, shine here to-day upon us.

In the sky's framework she has gleamed with
brightness :
The goddess has cast off the robe of darkness.
Rousing the world from sleep, with ruddy horses,
Dawn in her well-yoked chariot is arriving.

Bringing upon it many bounteous blessings,
Brightly she shines and spreads her brilliant lustre.
Last of innumerable morns departed,
First of bright morns to come has Dawn arisen.

Again and again newly born though ancient,
Decking her beauty with the self-same colours,
The goddess wastes away the life of mortals,
Like wealth diminished by the skilful player.

Gone are the mortals who in former ages
Beheld the flushing of the earlier morning.
We living men now look upon her shining;
Those will be born who shall hereafter see her.

The twin gods of morning, called Asvins or Horsemen, are the most frequently invoked among the deities of celestial light. They are the sons of Heaven, eternally young and handsome, at the yoking of whose car Ushas is born.

The importance of Indra, the favourite and national god of the Vedic Indian, is indicated by the fact that more than one-fourth of the *Rigveda* sings the praises of his greatness. Primarily a thunder-god, he constantly appears as vanquishing the demon of drought and darkness called Vritra, 'the Obstructor', setting free the waters or winning the light. This is the essence of the mythology of which he is the centre. The following stanzas illustrate his fight with the dragon:

I will proclaim the manly deeds of Indra,
The first that he performed, the lightning-wielder.
He smote the dragon, then discharged the waters,
And cleft the caverns of the lofty mountains.

Him lightning then availed not, nor thunder,
Nor mist, nor hailstorm that he spread around him.
When Indra and the dragon strove in battle,
The Bounteous god gained victory for ever.

Plunged in the midst of never-ceasing torrents,
That stand not still, but ever hasten onward,
The waters bore off Vritra's hidden body:
Indra's fierce foe sank down to lasting darkness.

Indra thus became the god of battle who aided the invading Aryans in their conflicts with the aborigines. His combats are often called *gav-isti* (literally 'desire of cows'), equivalent in meaning to 'cattle-raid'.

The following is a stanza celebrating Indra's greatness:

Both Heaven and Earth themselves bow down before him;
Before his might the very mountains tremble.
Who, known as Soma-drinker, armed with lightning,
Is wielder of the bolt: he, men, is Indra.

Though historically the most important of the solar deities, because in his later development he became one of the two chief gods of modern Hinduism, Vishnu occupies a very subordinate position in the *Rigveda*. He is invoked in few hymns, and little is said about him except that he takes three strides. This action is his characteristic trait, which doubtless represents the course of the sun through the three divisions of the universe. Later, in the Brahmanas, can be traced the development of the trait of benevolence, which culminates in the doctrine of his Avatars ('descents to earth') or incarnations which he assumed for the good of humanity.

The god Rudra occupies a curiously parallel position to Vishnu in the history of Indian religion. For while he is invoked as seldom as Vishnu in the *Rigveda,* he later becomes the other chief god in Hinduism. But while the goodwill of Vishnu is conspicuous, Rudra is the only god whose malevolence is already characteristic, and later becomes even more prominent. The hymns addressed to him mainly express fear of his terrible shafts and deprecation of his anger.

In the post-Vedic period he appears under the regular name of Siva, a euphemistic epithet meaning 'auspicious', and already applied to him in the *Rigveda.* Rudra is, of course, not purely malevolent like a demon. For he is besought not only to preserve from calamity, but to bestow welfare and healing on man and beast. This is, no doubt, only an euphemistic way of alluding to the injurious side of his activities.

His sons are the Maruts, or Storm-gods, a group of youthful warriors, variously referred to as twenty-one or sixty in number, the track of whose car is brilliant with lightnings:

They gleam with armlets as the heavens are decked with stars;
Like cloud-born lightnings shine the torrents of their rain.

Their onset is terrible when they cause the hills to quake:

The Maruts spread the mist abroad
And make the mountains rock and reel,
When with the winds they speed along;

and shatter the forests:

Before you, fierce ones, even woods bow down in fear,
The Earth herself, the very mountains tremble.

Parjanya, whose name in several passages simply means 'rain-cloud', and whose rudimentary personification is closely connected with the phenomena of the rain-storm, is characteristically a shedder of rain:

Like charioteer, his horses lashing with a whip,
The god makes manifest his messengers of rain.
From far away the roaring of the lion sounds,
What time Parjanya veils the firmament with rain.

The winds blow forth; to earth the quivering lightnings fall.
The plants shoot up; with moisture streams the realm of light.
For all the world abundant nourishment is born,
When by Parjanya Earth is fertilized with seed.

The Waters (Apas), who are regarded as aerial, not terrestrial divinities, are goddesses that come to the sacrifice and bestow boons. They are described as young wives, especially of Agni, the 'son of (the celestial) waters'. They cleanse not only from defilement, but even from moral guilt, bestowing remedies, long life, and immortality.

The Importance of Agni

Agni is by far the most important of the terrestrial deities. Next to Indra, he is the most frequently invoked of the Vedic gods, for about one-fifth of the hymns of the *Rigveda* are addressed to him. Since the priestly singers were in such close touch with him in his elemental form as the centre of the Vedic ritual, his anthropomorphism is still somewhat undeveloped. His name, too, Agni (Lat. *igni-s*), being the ordinary designation of the element, would naturally retard that process. His bodily parts are clearly connected with the various aspects of fire; thus, he is 'flame-haired'; and his teeth, jaws, and tongues evidently allude to the action of burning. He rides on a brilliant car, for he is the charioteer of sacrifice. The poets constantly dwell on his ritual aspects: thus, they often allude to his daily production from the two fire-sticks by means of friction. They are his parents who generate him as a new-born infant hard to catch. From the dry wood the god is born living; the child as soon as born devours his parents.

Reference is often made to Agni's threefold character or origin on earth (terrestrial fire), in the atmosphere (lightning), and in heaven (the sun). This Vedic triad may be the historical progenitor of the later Hindu Trinity of Brahma, Vishnu, and Siva. It may also have suggested the division of a single sacrificial fire into the three which form an essential feature of the cult of the Brahmanas.

As perpetually concerned with the sacrifice, Agni is mythologically the great priest, just as Indra is the great warrior.

A feature more characteristic of Agni than of any other Vedic deity is that of warding off evil spirits and hostile magic. As the Soma sacrifice forms, beside the fire-cult, a main feature in the ritual of the *Rigveda,* the personified Soma plant is naturally one of its leading deities. Judged by the number of hymns addressed to him (120), he comes next in importance to Agni. Since the Soma plant and its juice are pressed and offered by the priests as they invoke the god, the personification of Soma is undeveloped, as in the case of Agni. He is called the king of plants, and is often referred to as growing on the mountains. But heaven is regarded as his original and true home; and the myth of his having been brought down from thence by an eagle is frequently mentioned.

The hymns to Soma consist mostly of incantations chanted while the stalks of the plant are being pounded with stones, and the juice, as it passes through woollen strainers, flows into wooden vats, in which it is offered to the gods on the sacred grass. These processes are described with endless variety in obscure and mystical imagery.

In a few of the latest hymns of the *Rigveda* Soma begins to be mystically identified with the moon. In several passages of the *Atharvaveda* Soma actually means the moon. This identification is a commonplace of the Brahmanas, which explain the waning of the moon as the result of the ambrosia of which it consists being consumed by the gods and fathers. In post-Vedic literature Soma is a regular name of the moon. The starting-point of this remarkable development of meaning is doubtless to be found in the exaggerated terms with which the poets of the *Rigveda* describe the celestial nature and the brilliance of Soma.

Because of the mental exaltation produced by the beverage, Soma is regarded as a drink bestowing immortal life and is called the draught of immortality (*amrita*). The god is thus described as an awakener of eager thought, as a generator of hymns, a leader of poets.

The following stanzas illustrate the stimulating aspect

of this ritual divinity:

I have partaken wisely of the sweet food,
That stirs good thoughts, best banisher of trouble,
The food round which all deities and mortals,
Calling it honey-mead, collect together.

We have drunk Soma and become immortal;
We have attained the light the gods discovered.
What can hostility now do against us?
And what, immortal god, the spite of mortals?

Of this thy juice, pressed out with mind devoted,
We would partake as of paternal riches.
Prolong the years of life for us, king Soma,
As Surya lengthens out the days of spring-time.

Soma was not a creation of Vedic ritual. For both the plant and its deification were important features of the cult and mythology of the Indo-Iranian period, as there are many points of agreement in these respects between the *Rigveda* and the *Avesta.*

The belief in an intoxicating divine beverage, the home of which was in heaven, goes back, in fact, to the Indo-European period, when it must have been regarded as a kind of honey-mead (Sanskrit *madhu,* honey; Greek μεθυ, wine; Anglo-Saxon *medu,* mead).

Towards the end of the Rigvedic period the thought of the singers shows a tendency to advance from the concrete to the abstract. This movement resulted in the creation of abstract deities, of which some seven or eight, being personifications of abstract nouns, are found in the last book of the *Rigveda.* Such are Sraddha, 'Faith', and Manyu, 'Wrath'. These become commoner in the later Vedas. Thus, in the *Atharvaveda* appears the personification Kama, 'Desire', who in post-Vedic mythology becomes the Hindu Cupid, the flower-arrowed god of love.

Another and more numerous class seems to have originated in epithets which were applicable to older deities, but which acquired an independent value as the want of a god exercising the particular activity in question made itself felt. Such is Prajapati, 'Lord of Creatures', originally an epithet of gods like Savitar and Soma, who appears, in a later verse of the last book of the *Rigveda,* as distinct deity in the character of a creator. He is, in the *Atharvaveda* and the *Yajurveda* often, and in the Brahmanas regularly, recognized as the chief god. In the Sutras he is identified with Brahma, who becomes his successor in the post-Vedic age.

Deities in Pairs

A peculiarity of the Vedic religion is the invocation of pairs of deities whose names are associated in the form of dual compounds. There are about twenty-four of these pairs in the *Rigveda,* as *Mitra-Varuna,* that is, 'Mitra and Varuna'. The prototype of this class was probably *Dyava-Prithivi,* or 'Heaven and Earth', the universal parents.

Some deities appear in groups. The most numerous of these are the Maruts, who have already been mentioned, Another group consists of the Adityas, the sons of Aditi, seven or eight in number, whose chief is Varuna. There are besides some other colourless groups, such as the Vasus.

In addition to the higher gods, a number of lesser divinities appear in the *Rigveda.* The most prominent of these are the Ribhus, a deft-handed trio, who by their marvellous feats acquired immortality.

Not only do we find the great phenomena of nature invoked as divine powers in the *Rigveda,* but also various features of the earth's surface, as well as artificial objects. Besides Rivers and Waters, Mountains are often addressed as divinities, but only along with other natural objects or in association with gods. Plants are invoked as divine, chiefly with reference to their healing powers. Ritual implements, too, are deified, the most prominent among them being the sacrificial post and the pressing stones. Weapons also are sometimes addressed as divine.

Beside the celestial gods, demons often play a part in the *Rigveda.* Among these, two classes must be distinguished. The higher and more powerful kind fight against the gods in aerial combat. The typical conflict is that between Indra and the demon of drought, Vritra, the 'encompasser' of the waters, who is often described as a serpent (*ahi*). The lower class comprises terrestrial goblins, the enemies of men. They are usually called *raksas* and appear as obstructors of the sacrifice.

Worldly Hymns

About thirty hymns of the *Rigveda* are not concerned with the worship of gods or deified objects. Some twelve of these, nearly all occurring in the last book, are magical in character, like those of the *Atharvaveda,* such as spells directed against disease. One of them is addressed to frogs as bringers of rain. Here are two of its stanzas:

Resting in silence for a year,
Like Brahmins practising a vow,
The Frogs have lifted up their voice,
Excited by Parjanya's call.

As Brahmins at the mighty Soma offering
Sit round the large and brimming vessel talking:
So throng ye all around the pool to hallow
This annual day that, Frogs, begins the rain-time.

Hardly a score of the hymns are concerned with secular matters. They are of much interest as illustrating, apart from the religious hymns, the earliest thought and social life of India. One of the most important is a long wedding hymn. The following is one of its stanzas:

Free from the evil eye, thy husband hurting not,
Kind to our beasts, be friendly, full of energy;
Bear heroes, love the gods, and live in happiness;
Bring welfare to our bipeds and our quadrupeds.

One of the five funeral hymns is quite secular in tone, though a few of its stanzas mention the names of two or three of the gods. It supplies a good deal of information about the funeral customs of early Vedic India. Here are two of its stanzas:

Depart, O Death, along the furthest pathway,
Which is thine own, not that by mortals trodden.
I speak to thee that hast both sight and hearing:
Do not our offspring injure nor our heroes.

From the dead hand I take the bow he wielded,
To win for us dominion, might and glory.
Thou there, we here, rich in heroic offspring,
Will vanquish all assaults of every foeman.

Four hymns are didactic in character. One of them is a striking poem, in which a gambler laments the ruin brought on him by the irresistible lure of the dice. The following are three of its stanzas:

Downward they roll, then swiftly springing upward,
They overcome the man with hands, though
handless;
Cast on the board like magic bits of charcoal,
Though cold themselves, they burn the heart to
ashes.

It pains the gambler when he sees a woman,
Another's wife, and their well-ordered household.
He yokes those brown steeds early in the morning,
And when the fire is low sinks down a beggar.

'Play not with dice, but cultivate thy cornfield,
Enjoy thy riches, deeming them sufficient;
There are thy cows, there is thy wife, O Gambler':
This counsel Savitar the noble gives me.

The other three didactic hymns are forerunners of the sententious poetry for which post-Vedic literature is noted. The subject-matter of two other hymns is expressed in the form of riddles. One of these, for instance, speaks of the wheel of order with twelve spokes revolving round the heavens and containing within it, in couples, 720 sons. The allusion is evidently to the solar year with its twelve months comprising 360 days and 360 nights.

Besides what we learn from the comparatively few secular poems regarding the life and thought of those ancient times, the vast bulk of the hymns give us, as we have seen, a detailed account of the religious beliefs and practices of the earliest Indo-Aryans. But there are also many data incidentally scattered throughout these hymns, from which other information can be collected about their country and their manner of life.

Thus, we can infer with certainty what was the geographical area inhabited by the Indo-Aryans when the hymns of the *Rigveda* were composed. Of the twenty-five streams mentioned, only two or three did not belong to the Indus river-system. Their western boundary was evidently the Indus, if some of its western tributaries, such as the Kubha (Kabul) with its affluent the Suvastu (Swat) and the Gomati (Gomal) are included. On the east they extended to the Yamuna, the most westerly branch of the Gangetic system, though the Ganga (Ganges) itself was hardly known. On the north they were bounded by the mountains of the Himalaya, but on the south they had not yet spread to the Vindhya hills and the river Narmada, which separate north Hindustan from the southern triangle of the Deccan.

The evidence of rivers and mountains is corroborated by that of the flora and fauna mentioned. Thus the lotus, the names of which permeate the later Sanskrit poetry, is not used by the Vedic seers in their similes. The banyan tree and rice, so characteristic of eastern India, are unknown to the poets of the *Rigveda.* The lion is familiar, but the tiger is not mentioned in the hymns. The elephant, as its name, 'the animal with the hand' (*mrga hastin*), indicates, was still a novelty.

The Indo-Aryans were still moving eastwards, as conquering invaders, calling the aborigines unbelievers and 'black-skins'. As the cities and the great wealth of the latter are spoken of, they cannot have been nomads. The main occupation of the Aryans was warfare, in which they used chariots, bows and arrows, spears and axes. Their chief source of livelihood was cattle-breeding, but they practised agriculture also. For the eastern Punjab, where they chiefly dwelt, abounds in pastoral and agrarian land. Their food was mainly vegetarian. They ate meat, but only when animals were sacrificed.

The Value of Rigveda

Before leaving the *Rigveda* we may pause for a moment to answer the question that naturally arises: Is this work, so important in other respects, characterized by any literary merit worth mentioning? The answer is, that regarded from this aspect alone, its value is considerable. As is to be expected from its great antiquity, its diction is simpler and more natural than that of post-Vedic Sanskrit. Its hymns as a whole are composed with a surprising degree of metrical skill and command of language. As they were produced by a sacerdotal class, and were in general intended to accompany a ritual no longer primitive, their poetry is often impaired by conceits and mysticism, particularly where the two specifically ritual deities Agni and Soma are concerned. Yet **the hymns contain much genuine poetry often expressed in beautiful and even noble imagery,** as may perhaps be gathered from the few specimens translated above.

The Sama- and the Yajur-veda may be passed over, because the former, with the exception of a few verses, is entirely, and the latter as to more than one-fourth of its contents, derived from the Rigveda, and because both are concerned with the great sacrificial ceremonial. But the Atharvaveda calls for some attention. Its most salient feature is sorcery, which is directed mainly against hostile agencies, though a good many of its spells are also of an auspicious character, intended to secure health, long life, prosperity, and luck at gambling.

Contrasted with the *Rigveda,* the *Atharvaveda* consists for the most part of spells embodying popular magical notions that are concerned with demoniac powers and are of great antiquity. It also contains a large amount of theosophic and pantheistic matter representing a later stage of thought than the *Rigveda* does. With its 730 hymns and about 6,000 stanzas, its bulk amounts to not much more than one-half that of the *Rigveda*. A considerable part of the *Atharvaveda*, about one-sixth, is, as is also the case with the *Yajurveda*, written in prose.

Linguistically the *Atharvaveda* is decidedly later than the *Rigveda*, but earlier than the Brahmanas. It seems probable that its hymns, though some of them must be very old in matter, were not edited till after the Brahmanas of the *Rigveda* were composed.

The hostile charms of the *Atharvaveda* are largely directed against different diseases, or the demons supposed to cause them. These charms are accompanied by the employment of suitable herbs.

Hence the *Atharvaveda* is the oldest source of Indian medicine. The following is a charm against cough:

Just as the arrow sharpened well
Swift to a distance flies away,
So even thou, O cough, fly forth
Along the broad expanse of earth.

Another is meant to cure leprosy by the use of a dark-coloured plant:

Born in the night wast thou, O herb,
Dark-coloured, sable, black of hue:
Rich-tinted, tinge this leprosy,
And stain away its spots of grey!

A good many of these spells are imprecations against

foes and sorcerers:

Avoid and pass us by, O curse,
Even as a burning fire a pond.
Here strike him down that curses us,
As Heaven's lightning smites the tree.

Of the auspicious charms, many aim at the prolongation of life:

Rise up, O man, from here, and straightway casting
Death's fetters from thy feet, depart not downward;
From life upon this earth be not yet severed,
Nor from the sight of Agni and the sunlight.

Here is a spell to secure luck at play:

As at all times the lightning-stroke
Smites irresistibly the tree:
So gamesters with the dice would I
Beat irresistibly to-day.

The following stanzas are meant to secure victory in battle:

Arise and arm, ye spectral forms,
Followed by meteoric flames;
Ye serpents, spirits of the deep,
Demons of night, pursue our foes!

As birds start back affrighted at the falcon's cry,
As, day and night, they tremble at the lion's roar:
So thou, O drum, resound against our enemies,
Scare them away in terror, and confound their aims.

This is a stanza from a hymn meant to command

a woman's affection by the agency of Kama, god of desire:

With longing feathered, tipped with love,
Its shaft is formed of fixed desire:
With this his arrow levelled well
Shall Kama pierce thee to the heart.

There is one hymn which, though ending in two spells of the usual Atharvan type, describes in its preceding stanzas the omniscience of the god Varuna in an exalted strain, doubtless to emphasize the impossibility of any foe's escaping his vigilance:

This earth is all King Varuna's dominion,
And that broad sky whose boundaries are distant.
The loins of Varuna are these two oceans;
Yet in this drop of water he is hidden.

He that would flee afar beyond the heavens,
Could not escape King Varuna's attention:
His spies come hither, from the sky descending,
With all their thousand eyes the earth surveying.

King Varuna discerns all things existent
Between the earth and sky, and all beyond them.
The winkings of men's eyes by him are counted.
As gamesters dice, so he lays down his statutes.

3.

The Upanishads

THE poetical and creative period of the Vedas was followed by that of the Brahmanas, several of which are attached to the Vedas, but in both form and matter constitute an entirely different type of literature. Written throughout in prose of a clumsy kind, they are notable as representing the earliest Indo-European prose-writing, which is specially valuable in tracing the history of syntax. They are theological treatises analogous to the Hebrew Talmud as compared with the Old Testament. Being expositions of the sacrificial ceremonial, they explain it in minute detail, illustrating its value with numerous myths and speculations on its origin. As the most ancient literature on ritual, they contain much interesting material both for the student of the history of religion and of the history of Indian civilization.

In these works we find a definite development of the system of the four castes which form the basis of the almost innumerable castes and sub-castes into which the Hindu society of to-day is divided. In this system the priesthood, the holders of the secret, of the all-powerful sacrifice, gained the dominating position. These works also show the growth of a sacrificial ceremonial more elaborate and complex than any other the world has ever seen. They thus shed much light on the sacerdotalism of ancient India. One or more Brahmanas are attached to each Veda. They vary in age, as is shown by their internal linguistic evidence. The most important of them all is that which is attached to the White *Yajurveda:* the *Satapatha Brahmana,* or 'Brahmana of the Hundred Paths'. It is,next to the *Rigveda* and the *Atharvaveda,* the most valuable product of the Vedic age.

A later development of the Brahmanas are the Aranyakas or 'Forest Treatises', which constitute their concluding portions and are partly theosophic in character. They form a transition to the Upanishads, which are usually their final part. These Upanishads, or esoteric treatises, mark the last stage in the development of the Brahmana literature, being entirely concerned with theosophical speculations on the nature of things. The subject-matter of all the old Upanishads is essentially the same, consisting of speculations on the nature of the Supreme soul (*Atma* or *Brahma*).

That the Upanishads represent the latest phase of Vedic literature is corroborated by the fact that their language very closely approximates to the Classical Sanskrit of the post-Vedic age, which may be said to have assumed its permanent form about 500 B.C. The two most important of the Upanishads are the *Chandogya* of the *Samaveda* and the *Brhadaranyaka* of the White *Yajurveda.* About a dozen Upanishads stand out as the best, but there are many others of less value.

The Upanishads generally form a continuation of the Brahmanas on their speculative as contrasted with their ritual side. But they really expound a new religion which is opposed to the sacrificial ceremonial and has virtually represented the philosophic aspect of Hinduism for 2,500 years. They do not aim at securing earthly and afterwards heavenly bliss in the abode of Yama by sacrificing correctly to the gods, but at obtaining deliverance from mundane existence by the absorption of the individual soul in the world-soul through correct knowledge. Here, therefore, ritual appears as useless, and saving knowledge as all-important. The Upanishad conception of the world-soul (*Atma*) is the final development of the personal creator Prajapati, who has become the impersonal source of all being Brahma.

Atma and Brahma

Atman in the *Rigveda* means only 'breath'; in the Brahmanas it came to mean 'soul' and even to be attributed to the Universe, being said to 'pervade this Universe'. *Brahma* (neuter) in the *Rigveda* meant nothing more than 'devotion', 'prayer'; even in the oldest Brahmanas it already has the sense of 'universal holiness'; in the Upanishads, finally, it signifies the holy principle animating nature. Having a long subsequent development, this term is a very epitome of the evolution of religious thought in India. Atma and Brahma usually appear as synonyms in the Upanishads; but strictly speaking, Brahma is the cosmical principle pervading the universe, while Atma is the psychical principle in man. The *Brhadaranyaka Upanishad* describes Brahma negatively in an exhaustive manner, as without physical or other qualities, as immortal thinker and knower, as the eternal in which space is woven, and which is interwoven in it. **Here for the first time in the history of human thought the Absolute is grasped and definitely expressed.**

The following is an account of the Atman from a metrical Upanishad:

Its form can never be to sight apparent,
Not any one may with his eye behold it:
By heart and mind and soul alone they grasp it,
And those who know it thus, become immortal.

Since not by speech and not by thought,
Not by the eye can it be reached:
How else may it be understood
But only when one says 'it is'?

The notion that the material world is an illusion (*maya*), familiar in the later Vedanta philosophical system, is first met with in the *Svetasvatara,* one of the later Upanishads, though it is inherent even in the oldest. This is virtually identical with the teaching of Kant, that the things of experience are only phenomena of the thing in itself.

The fundamental doctrine of the Upanishads is the identity of the individual *atman* with the world *Atman.* It is expressed in the *Chandogya Upanisad* thus: 'This whole world consists of it: that is the real, that is the soul, that art thou, O Svetaketu.' All the teachings of the Upanishads are summed up in that famous formula, 'That art thou' (*tat tvam asi*).

Many metaphors are used to make clear the nature of the pantheistic self. Here is one: 'As a lump of salt, thrown into the water, would dissolve and could not be taken out again, while the water, wherever tasted, would be salt, so is this great being endless, unlimited, simply compacted of cognition. Arising out of these elements, it disappears again in them. After death there is no consciousness. This is further explained to mean that when the duality on which consciousness is based disappears, consciousness must necessarily cease.

Parallel with the doctrine of salvation depending on the knowledge that the individual soul is identical with the world soul was developed the theory of transmigration. In its earliest form it appears in the *Satapatha Brahmana,* where the notion occurs that retribution is inflicted in the next world in the guise of repeated births and deaths. It is developed in the Upanishads, where the fullest account given of it is this. The forest ascetic possessed of true knowledge enters, after death, the 'path of the gods', which leads to absorption in Brahma. But the householder who has performed sacrifice and good works goes by the 'path of the fathers' to the moon, where he remains till the results of his actions are exhausted. Then he returns to earth, where he is first born as a plant and afterwards as a man of one of the three highest castes. This is a double retribution: first in the celestial, then by transmigration in the terrestrial world. The former is a survival of the old Vedic belief regarding the future life, but it continues throughout later Hinduism along with terrestrial transmigration.

Transmigration

The theory of transmigration must have been firmly established by the time when Buddhism arose (*c.* 500 B.C.), for Buddha accepted it without question. A curious thing, however, is that he also adopted the doctrine of *karma* or 'action', which regulates the new birth as dependent on a man's own previous deeds, although he denied the existence of soul altogether; he thus assumed that *karma* continued to operate from one birth to another, though there was no soul to pass between them.

There are indications of a chronological nature that the latest Brahmanas were produced not long before the rise of Buddhism. The general evidence of the geographical data contained in the Brahmana literature points to its having grown up in the land of the Kuru-Panchalas, the region around the upper courses of the Jamuna and the Ganges. But the *Satapatha Brahmana* indicates that the Brahmanical system by the time this book was composed had spread to the east of Madhyadesa, the Midland, to Kosala with its capital Ayodhya, and to Videha (Tirhut) with its capital Mithila. There is some probability that the White *Yajurveda* was edited in this eastern region. Some allusions it contains indicate that the *Satapatha Brahmana* came into being shortly before Buddhism and the germs of the Sanskrit epics arose. Internal evidence also shows that it belongs to a late period of the Brahmana age. For its style is more lucid, its treatment of the sacrificial ritual is more methodical, and the idea of the unity of the universe is more developed than in any other Brahmana, while its Upanishad, the *Brhadaranyaka,* is the finest outcome of Vedic philosophy.

The Vedic period had now reached its final stage, the Upanishad literature of which supplies the unclarified theosophic doctrines that in the post-Vedic period developed into the pantheistic system called Vedanta, which has ever since remained the predominant philosophy of India. To the hymn collections of the four Vedas and their Brahmanas the expression Veda is alone applicable. These two literary phases combined correspond to what the Old Testament was among the Jews. They were regarded as authoritative, as the ultimate appeal, by all Hindu sects and systems of philosophy. They were after the close of the Vedic period thought to be revealed, and were called by the name of *Sruti* or 'hearing' because the sacred texts were not written, but recited and heard. They were believed to have been emitted by the god Brahma and 'seen' (not composed) by the seers of old.

The Language

During the whole of the Vedic period there was, apart from the non-Aryan tongues that must have prevailed in the area of India, only one Aryan, the Vedic language, at least as preserved in literary records. This language remains almost changeless, as far as its phonetic aspect is concerned, throughout the Vedic period. But in grammar and vocabulary considerable change may be traced between the beginning and the end of this period. The wealth and variety of nominal and verbal forms tended to diminish and to approach the greater uniformity and regularity of Classical Sanskrit. Not only, however, do the Vedic texts furnish traces of the existence of contemporary vernacular words cognate to the literary language, but the knowledge that Buddha by the end of the Vedic period already used a vernacular dialect in order to be understood by the people, besides the evidence of the Asoka inscriptions from *c.* 250 B.C., show that popular Aryan dialects must have been developing long before 500 B.C.

The hymns of the Vedas composed in the earliest form of Sanskrit were handed down orally for many centuries by families of priestly singers. It was not till towards the end of the Vedic period that writing became known in India. There is no proof of its existence there till the third century B.C. in the reign of the Buddhist king Asoka, who caused religious edicts to be inscribed on rocks and pillars all over the country. Many of these have been discovered, deciphered, and published. Minute palaeographical investigations made towards the end of last century have shown that the script here used is derived from the oldest form of northern Semitic writing that appears in Phoenician inscriptions and on the Moabite stone which was inscribed about 890 B.C.

This may have been introduced by traders perhaps as early as 800 B.C., but its use was doubtless long limited to commercial requirements such as accounts and then employed in the chancelleries for documents of various kinds. But the writing of the third century shows that it must have undergone a long-continued elaboration by grammarians who adapted an alphabet of twenty-two letters to the phonetic needs of Sanskrit which already had forty-four sounds. The right-to-left direction of the Semitic script had been reversed in the Asoka inscriptions. By the fourth century B.C. at the latest, the letters of this alphabet had already been arranged and classified phonetically as we know from the great Sanskrit grammar of Panini, whose work cannot be dated later than the fourth century. Here the vowels come first (*a, i, u,* etc.), then the consonants in groups according to the organ (guttural, palatal, etc.) with which they are pronounced.

The same Semitic writing is the source of the Greek alphabet which, through Latin, has come down to us, and which still retains the unscientific order of the letters derived from the Semitic script. The Latin name of the list of letters, *alpha-betum,* which we have adopted, represents the first two Greek, borrowed from the first two Semitic letters *aleph* (hieroglyphic for ox = *a*) and *beth* (hieroglyphic for house = *b*). Thus our own word *alphabet* contains perhaps more of the history of civilization than any other word in the language. From this early Sanskrit writing are derived all the numerous other scripts prevalent in India, however much they may differ at the present day.

We do not know when the alphabet first began to be used in India to write down texts. In the whole of ancient (Vedic) literature no evidence can be produced that writing was known. Buddhism arose about 500 B.C., and its sacred canon was probably completed by 400 B.C. But though we here find a good deal to prove a knowledge of writing and of its extensive use at that time, there is no mention of manuscripts nor of the reading or copying of sacred texts. The explanation of this is that all the early literature was produced orally and handed down orally. This had been an established custom for centuries from the earliest times. Thus the memories of learned priests were, instead of libraries, the repositories of literature. Even in the last centuries B.C. works on grammar and phonetics make no reference to written letters, but only to spoken sounds, and the whole grammatical terminology is concerned with the spoken word only, never with written texts. On the other hand, a few centuries after the beginning of our era the copying and presenting of books are often praised.

Hence it is probable that written books really did not exist in the centuries before our era. Yet it seems strange at first sight that writing should have been known for centuries without having been applied to literary purposes. The oral tradition of sacred texts was, however, so well established a habit, that the substitution of any other method would not suggest itself as necessary. It was, in fact, in the interest of the priests who were the custodians of the sacred texts to withhold them from unauthorized persons by not writing them down. We are, moreover, continually told in the early literature that whoever wished to learn any branch of knowledge had to betake himself to a teacher and to acquire it by listening to him and not to do so in any other way. Indeed oral tradition offered a better guarantee for the preservation of the original text than the repeated copying of manuscripts. Thus the hymns of the oldest sacred text, the *Rigveda,* have been preserved entirely unchanged for 3,000 years, whereas later works, dating from a period when writing was widely used for literary purposes, have been so much changed that it has in many cases been critically impossible to restore such texts to their original form.

The evidence of manuscripts themselves as to the age of writing in India does not carry us very far back, owing to the unsuitableness of the Indian climate for their preservation. Manuscripts of the thirteenth century A.D. are very rare; extremely few have been discovered in India dating from the twelfth; and only one from the eleventh century. Outside India older specimens have been found: in Nepal, some going back to the tenth century; in Japan, others to the sixth; and in Central Asia a few have turned up belonging to the fifth century. In Chinese Turkistan wooden tablets with Sanskrit writing, which must be as old as 300 A.D., have been dug out of the sands of the desert. The earliest material used for writing in India was palm-leaves; and although paper, which is much more convenient, was introduced with the Muhammadan conquest from about 1000 A.D., manuscripts continued to be written on birch-bark till about 200 years ago, and palm-leaves are still often employed for writing on in different parts of the country, and their use for this purpose can be traced as far back as the first century A.D. in India.

Besides these, wood, leather, metal, and stone were sometimes, though rarely, employed as writing material in early times. Copper-plates were occasionally used for this purpose, perhaps from about 100 A.D. Sanskrit dramas have been found engraved even on rocks. But Sanskrit texts have mostly been written on paper since the Muhammadan conquest. The oldest known paper manuscript found in India dates from soon after 1200 A.D.

Some centuries after the beginning of our era, libraries as the depositories of Sanskrit manuscripts came into existence in temples, monasteries, the palaces of kings, and the houses of the wealthy. The evidence of his works shows that a Sanskrit poet who lived at the beginning of the seventh century must have possessed a large library. In the eleventh century a famous library was owned by a king named Bhoja of Dhar in the west of India. In the course of centuries large libraries were formed, so that each of the collections at Tanjore, Madras, Poona, Benares, and Calcutta consists at the present time of more than 12,000 manuscripts. In the Bodleian Library at Oxford, Sanskrit manuscripts have in the course of the last hundred years accumulated to the number of nearly 10,000. There are also several other smaller, though considerable collections of Sanskrit manuscripts in the libraries of European capitals. Practically the whole of this vast mass of manuscripts representing Sanskrit literature has been made accessible through catalogues compiled by the directions of librarians in Europe or by the order of the Indian Government, which since 1868 has made a considerable annual grant towards the search for, and the purchase of, Sanskrit manuscripts.

Indian literature is for the most part written in

Sanskrit, but in its widest sense it comprises also writings in many Indo-Aryan and some Dravidian languages. It may as a whole be divided into three periods: (1) Ancient Indian, composed or written in an early form of Sanskrit; (2) Medieval Indian, written in Classical Sanskrit and in daughter languages derived from Sanskrit and called Prakrit; and (3) Modern Indian, written in the languages spoken in India at the present day.

At the end of the later Vedic period a new era in the history of Indian civilization was about to appear in the rise of new forms of literature, language, and religion.

4.

Sutras, Buddhism and Jainism

The new literary period of India which now opens out has a dual character, both in its linguistic and its religious aspect. It was now that the ancient Indo-Aryan language reached its final stage, assuming, by the elaboration of grammarians, the form known as Sanskrit, which has remained for more than 2,000 years the unchanging literary vehicle of the religion of the Hindus. In this earliest period of Sanskrit were composed the Sutras, concise treatises in which the religion of the Brahmanas, on its ritual side, was systematically condensed with a view to preserving the ancient sacerdotal literature. They were never regarded as sacred, but were felt to be treatises compiled with the help of oral priestly tradition from the contents of the Brahmanas solely to meet practical needs.

The oldest of the Sutras seem to go back to about the time when Buddhism arose. It is, in fact, not improbable that the rise of the new religion gave the first impulse to the composition of systematic manuals of Brahminic worship. This literature has a style of its own, consisting of brief rules strung together (*sutra* 'thread'). The Sutras may be divided into three classes. The first of these comprises the Srauta Sutras, which are concerned with the sacrificial aspect of a particular school attached to any one of the Vedas. They are in fact, technical guides to the Vedic sacrifice. There are about twelve of these ritual treatises.

Another class is the Grihya Sutras or domestic rules for the many ceremonies applicable to the life of the Hindu from birth to death. These are of unequalled importance for the history and ethnology of the age, forming a useful supplement to the contents of the *Atharvaveda.* More than a dozen of this type of Sutra are extant. One of the most important is the *Kausika Sutra* which, besides treating of the domestic ritual, deals with the magical and medicinal practices belonging specially to the sphere of the *Atharvaveda.* An interesting rite handled by these works is that of initiation (*upanayana*), called the second birth, of boys when they are invested with the sacred cord admitting them to Vedic study. It is a modification of the very ancient and primitive ceremony of initiation on the attainment of manhood. Other ceremonies of much interest are the wedding and the funeral rites, many elements of which survive in India down to the present day.

The third and last class of Sutras are the Dharma Sutras, which are concerned with the customs of everyday life, and constitute the earliest Indian legal works. They deal fully with the religious, but only briefly and partially with the secular side of law. Only some half-dozen of them have survived. Among other subjects they deal with the duties of kings, criminal justice, the laws of inheritance, and of marriage. The oldest, the law-book of Gautama, is composed entirely in prose aphorisms. Among these legal treatises must have been included a *Manava Dharma-sutra,* forming the basis of the famous later and still extant metrical law-book, the *Code of Manu.*

According to the Indian traditional view, the whole body of auxiliary works bearing on the Veda and composed in the Sutra style form six classes called *vedangas,* or 'limbs of the Veda', comprising the subjects of religious practice, phonetics, grammar, etymology, metre, and astronomy. They all aim at explaining, preserving, or practically applying the sacred texts. **Of the greatest interest in these groups are the linguistic works which deal with phonetics, derivation, and grammar; for in these subjects the Indians arrived at more important results than any other nation of antiquity.** One of the most important books produced in this period is the *Nirukta* of Yaska, which besides being of great value from the point of view of exegesis and grammar, is highly interesting as the earliest specimen of Sanskrit prose of the classical type, which is somewhat anterior to the date of Panini himself. It should undoubtedly be attributed to the beginning of the Sutra period. The great grammar of Panini comes later in this period, not earlier than the fifth century B.C.; but it must be regarded as the virtual starting-point of the post-Vedic age, for it almost entirely dominates the whole of the subsequent Sanskrit literature. Regarded as an infallible authority, Panini superseded his predecessors, all of whom except Yaska have disappeared.

To the Sutras is attached a very large supplementary literature consisting chiefly of manuals, called Prayogas or Paddhatis, which deal with the sacrificial ceremonial. There is here also a group of Vedic Indexes called

Anukramanis, which give lists of the hymns quoted by their initial words, and of their authors, metres, and deities, in the order in which these hymns occur in the various Samhitas. One of these indexes supplies the number of stanzas, words, and syllables contained in the *Rigveda*.

By the beginning of this period (500 B.C.) the Sanskrit language reached its final development. This was of a negative character, consisting not of growth, but of decay by loss of grammatical forms. Any indications of the nature of growth were limited to the extended employment of periphrastic forms, of compound and adverbial, in place of primary prepositions, and, in syntax, of the use of past participles for finite tenses, and of long compounds. But a fixed grammatical standard was not attained till the appearance of Panini's work, which completely arrested the development of the language. Henceforward it remained the unchanging vehicle of the Brahmin religion.

Buddhism

During the whole of this period, however, there existed a vernacular, descended from a Vedic dialect and remaining parallel with Sanskrit, as the vehicle of Buddhism and bearing the designation of Prakrit. While Sanskrit remained the language of orthodoxy, Prakrit became that of heterodoxy in the two new religions of Jainism and Buddhism, which arose much about the same time and at the beginning of this period (*c.* 500 B.C.). The relation of this language to Sanskrit resembles that of old Italian to Classical Latin, being characterized by the avoidance of conjunct consonants (which are assimilated) and of final consonants, as in *sutta,* compared with Sanskrit *sutra,* 'thread', and *vijju,* with *vidyut,* 'lightning'. The oldest literary form of Prakrit is Pali. In this language the sacred canon of Buddhism, in its oldest form, has been handed down.

This Pali canon, though composed in the north of India, has been preserved only in Ceylon, Burma, and Siam. It contains the doctrine of the older school, called *Hinayana*, 'the lesser vehicle', the chief aim of which is to obtain *Nirvana* ('extinction') or release of the individual from suffering. No work of Buddhist literature goes back to Buddha's time, but much contained in the canon, such as the famous sermon of Benares, may preserve the actual words spoken by Buddha. Almost the whole of the earliest Buddhist literature consists of short collections in the form of speeches, poems, tales, rules of conduct, gathered together in larger collections called *pitakas* or 'baskets', three of which combined form the Pali canon (*tipitaka*). This canon, first constituted in the third century B.C. during the reign of the Buddhist king Asoka in India, was fixed in the first century B.C. in Ceylon. The *Tipitaka* has, on the whole, since then been handed down with great care; but it must have undergone some modifications, for several contradictions which it contains could not otherwise be accounted for. The main contents of the three 'baskets' are the following:

1. The first is concerned with the discipline and the daily life of the Buddhist order.

2. The second, consisting of five collections of lectures, describes the religion of Buddha and his earliest disciples. One of its topics deals with a large number of Brahmin occupations from which the Buddhist monk should refrain. It also treats of the relations of Brahmanism and Buddhism, contrasting the cult of the followers of

the three Vedas with Buddhist ideals. It, moreover, describes the 'complete nirvana' (*parinibbana*), which is a continuous account of the last days of Buddha. There are further sermons which throw light not only on the life of Buddhist monks, but on Brahmin sacrifices, on forms of asceticism, and on the relations of Buddha to the Jains.

The fifth section in this *Pitaka* 'the collection of small pieces', is later than the rest. Being composed chiefly in verse, it contains all the most important works of Indian Buddhist poetry. One of the works in it is the *Metta-sutta,* in which kindness towards all creatures is praised as the true Buddhist cult. Another work in this *Pitaka,* the *Dhamma-pada,* or 'Words of Religion', being an anthology of Buddhist ethical maxims, is the most famous product of Buddhist literature. The *Itivuttaka* (The Book of 'Thus he hath spoken'), which is composed in prose and verse, is a collection of the sayings of Buddha. The *Thera-gatha* and the *Theri-gatha,* or 'Songs of Monks and Nuns', are fine poems exalting mental calm as the religious ideal of Buddhism.

One of the most interesting books here is the *Jataka,* a collection of about 550 stories of former existences of Buddha in the character of a future saviour.

3. The third *Pitaka* is concerned with *abhidhamma* or 'higher religion', dealing with the same matter as the second *Pitaka,* but in a more scholastic manner. As it is composed mostly in the form of question and answer, it resembles a catechism.

The Pali canon, apart from additions, was entirely composed in India. But the non-canonical literature was produced by Buddhist monks in Ceylon; the only important exception here being the *Milinda-panha,* or 'Questions of Menander'. This work was evidently written in northwestern India. It is a dialogue represented as taking place between a Buddhist teacher and the Greek king Menander who in the first century B.C. ruled over the Indus territory, Gujarat, and the valley of the Ganges. The original part of this work was probably written about the beginning of the Christian era.

Pali Buddhism represents the doctrine called the *Hina-yana*, or 'Little Vehicle'. There was also a Sanskrit canon which followed this doctrine, but only fragmentary parts of three books, one of which is the *Dharma-pada,* have as yet been discovered. A work representing this doctrine is the *Mahavastu* or 'Book of Great Events'. Its chief content is a miraculous biography of Buddha written in 'mixed Sanskrit'. It is of great importance as containing many old versions of texts that also occur in the Pali canon, such as the 'Sermon of Benares' and a section of the *Dhamma-pada.* Many of the Jatakas are also found in it. Some traces appear in this work of its having been influenced by the *Mahayana* doctrines. The nucleus of the book probably dates from the second century B.C., though it contains some much later additions. There are several other Buddhist Hinayana works in Sanskrit, which, though not coming within the limits of this period, may most conveniently be mentioned here.

The *Lalita-vistara,* a biography of Buddha, is a continuous narrative in Sanskrit prose interspersed with long metrical pieces in what is called 'mixed Sanskrit'. As its original part was extended in a *Mahayana* sense, it contains both old and new elements. It is thus of interest as presenting the development of the Buddha legend from its earliest beginnings to the deification of Buddha as a god above all gods.

The *Buddha-carita,* or 'Life of Buddha', is an epic in pure Sanskrit, which must have been composed about 100 A.D. It does not contain any pronounced Mahayana doctrine.

Another work, dating probably from the fourth century A.D. is the *Jataka-mala.* It contains thirty-four stories nearly all of which are found in the Pali *Jataka* book. Written in a mixture of verse and prose, it conforms in language and style to the standard of Classical Sanskrit.

Cognate with these works are several collections called *Avadanas,* 'Stories of Great Deeds', which are practically Jatakas. One of these is the *Avadana-sataka,* or 'Century of Great Deeds' which probably dates from the second century A.D. and contains pieces from the Sanskrit canon. Another is the *Divyavadana,* or 'Heavenly Stories of Great Deeds'. This work often mentions the Sanskrit canon, besides having several legends in common with the Pali canon.

Mahayana

The great majority of the Sanskrit Buddhists belonged to the new school of the *Mahayana* or 'Great Vehicle', the chief aim of which was to attain the condition of a Bodhisattva, or future Buddha, who brings *Nirvana* within the reach of the entire human race. This school, though possessing no canon has nine religious texts called *dharmas.* Its most important work is the *Saddharma-pundarika,* 'The Lotus of Good Religion'. It is written in Sanskrit prose interspersed with *gathas* in 'mixed Sanskrit'. In its earliest form it dates from about 200 A.D. Buddha is here no longer a man, who in the Pali *suttas* was a mendicant, but a god above all gods, who has lived for countless ages and will live for ever in the future as well. His doctrine is that every man can become a Buddha by performing meritorious works and leading a moral life.

Later is the *Karanda-vyuha,* which is akin to the Hindu Puranas, exalting Avalokitesvara, 'The Bodhisattva who Looks Down' with infinite pity on all beings, refusing Buddhahood till all are saved. The yearning for salvation has probably never been more powerfully expressed than in this compassionate figure of Buddhism. His cult is known to have existed before 400 A.D.

The Mahayana doctrine was systematized by Nagarjuna, once a Brahmin, who flourished about 300 A.D. Mahayana texts were translated into Chinese in the third century A.D., and the Gandhara type of Buddhist art, which illustrates the Mahayana doctrine, came into being about the beginning of our era. Asanga, the son of a Brahmin from Peshawar, who flourished about 300 to 350 A.D., introduced the practice of Yoga into the Mahayana doctrine.

From about 600 A.D. Buddhism began to decay in India, as is shown by the approximation of its later literature to that of the Hindu Puranas. Not only are Hindu deities such as Vishnu and Siva, Sarasvati and Mahadevi introduced, but also magical spells, which at first containing Buddhist doctrine, finally degenerated into pure gibberish.

The last stage in'the degradation of Indian Buddhism is to be found in the Buddhist Tantras, treatises composed in barbarous Sanskrit. Most of them are connected with Yoga, which aims at the highest knowledge of 'nothingness'. The teaching and practice of this *yoga* are a mixture of mysticism, sorcery, and erotics, accompanied by disgusting orgies. These Tantras have no longer any connexion with Buddhism beyond being described as 'promulgated by Buddha'. They do not differ from the Saivite Tantras, for they inculcate the worship of the linga and of Saivite gods, besides introducing many female deities into their cult.

Religious Art

Without the evidence of the religious art of Buddhism, neither the history of that faith nor even of Indian religion in general could be fully understood. In the first period of Buddhism, when the *Hinayana* doctrine prevailed, the earliest architectural and plastic religious art of India arose. The reign of Asoka (272-231 B.C.), whose rule extended practically over the whole of India, except the extreme south, is the starting-point of the history of Indian art. Stone then first began to be used in structural monuments.

The earliest of these were *stupas* or hemispherical burial-mounds, commemorative of Buddha, and enclosing relics of the founder of the faith. The best preserved and one of the oldest surviving *stupas* is at Sanchi in central India. The hemisphere is built of brick, but the surrounding rail and the four gateways in it consist of stone, though clearly imitations of wooden structures. On the top of the dome was a boxlike structure surmounted by an umbrella, the Indian emblem of sovereignty and symbolical of Buddha's princely descent. This crowning feature, usually called a 'tee', has disappeared from all the structural Indian *stupas,* but its form can be seen in the sculptural representations of it in the interior or on the facade of rock-cut temples or on the surrounding rail of structural *stupas*. The *stupa* has had an interesting development in later Indian and Chinese architecture; and its gateway (*torana*) was intrpduced with Buddhism into other Asiatic countries from India.

Another class of Buddhist architecture was the *chaitya* or assembly hall, the exact counterpart of the Christian Church, not only in form. but in use. Till recent times only rock-cut examples were known in India. The typical *chaitya* consists of a nave and of side aisles terminating in an apse or semi-dome. The pillars separating the nave from the aisles are continued round the apse. Under the latter and in front of its pillars is a rock-cut *stupa* serving as an object of adoration by circumambulation. It occupies nearly the same position as the altar does in a Christian church. The tee was doubtless usually surmounted by a wooden umbrella, but it has everywhere disappeared except at Karli, the finest *chaitya* cave in India. The excavation of these rock-cut assembly halls extended from about 250 B.C. to 600 A.D.

A third architectural class arose in the form of *viharas* or monasteries as residences for Buddhist monks. Nearly 1,000 rock-cut specimens are to be found in India, almost all situated in the west, chiefly at Ajanta, Nasik, and Ellora. They generally consist of a hall, surrounding which are a number of excavated sleeping cubicles. The latter in the oldest *viharas* usually contain a stone bed. About forty of the western monasteries were probably excavated before the Christian era.

Hinayana

Down to the middle of the first century of our era the Buddhist cult followed the doctrine of the *Hinayana,* in which there was no worship of Buddha, and no figure of him appeared in sculptural art. Reverence at that time was paid to relics, *stupas,* bo-trees, footprints of Buddha, and sacred symbols such as the trident (*trisul*) and the wheel of the law (*cakra*). These are constantly represented as adored by men and even animals in the sculptures of the period at Bharhut, Sanchi, Bodh Gaya, and in the assembly halls and monasteries of the West. But no figure of Buddha sculptured in India can be dated earlier than about 100 A.D. It was, then, in the beginning of the second period of Buddhist religious art, the epoch of the *Mahayana* school, that statues of Buddha appeared in the ancient province of Gandhara, the modern Yusufzai country and the neighbouring valleys of the Kabul and the Swat. Here was created the conventional type of Buddha, a seated cross-legged figure adorned with a halo. From this centre it spread to other parts of India, and was finally diffused all over the Buddhist world.

Jainism

In the same century (the sixth) as Buddhism, but somewhat earlier, was established the religious system of Jainism. Equally an offshoot of Brahminism, it was, as denying the authority of the Veda, similarly regarded by the Brahmins as heretical. It is, like Buddhism, a monastic and pessimistic religion. It looks upon life in the world, perpetuated by the transmigration of the soul, as an evil; and it aims at gaining liberation that puts an end to the cycle of births, by the attainment of right knowledge. Like Buddhism and the Hindu Sankhya system, Jainism is atheistic, denying the existence of an absolute supreme god. As both Jainism and Buddhism are monastic systems outside the pale of Brahmanism, and have several external resemblances, it was at one time held by scholars that the former was an offshoot of the latter. But the erroneousness of this theory has since been proved; for the canonical Buddhist books often mention the Jains as a rival sect, besides agreeing with Jain tradition in naming the same place as the locality where Mahavira, the founder of Jainism, died. It has been shown that Mahavira was a slightly older contemporary of Buddha. He may have been only the reformer of a sect originated by a predecessor named Parsva. But there is no documentary evidence proving that the latter was an historical person.

The account of Mahavira's life in the canonical books of the Jains may be regarded as having an historical foundation. It is this. Belonging to the military clan called Jnata, he was born near the town of Vaisali, 27 miles north of Patna. His parents having died when he was thirty, he became a monk, and entered upon a course of self-mortification lasting twelve years, when he reached the state of omniscience (*kaivalya,* which 'is equivalent to the Buddhist *bodhi* or 'enlightenment'). At the age of seventy-two he died (*c.* 480 B.C.) at Pava.

Both Mahavira and the preceding twenty-three mythical patriarchs (*tirthankaras*) of Jainism came to be adored as gods (*devas*) and to have erected to them temples in which their idols were worshipped. Mention is already made in some of the canonical books of this worship, which was fully developed in the first centuries of our era.

Jainism in the first century A.D., split into two sects called the Svetambaras ('white-robed'), and the Digambaras ('sky-clad') who went about stark naked till the Muhammadans compelled them to wear a minimum of clothing. The texts of the Jain religion are composed in a dry didactic style. As they contain little of general human interest, they need only be briefly described here. The Jains designate their complete sacred books by the terms *Siddhanta* or *Agama.* They call the first and most important part of their canon the twelve Angas ('members' of their religion). The whole canon was edited by Devarddhi Gani in 454 A.D., having till then been handed down by oral tradition.

The language in which it is composed the Jains call *Ardha-magadhi* ('half-magadhi') and is that in which Mahavira is said to have preached. But as the texts show signs of having been modernized in the process of oral transmission, it is best to call the language of the sacred texts Jain Prakrit. Quite different from this language is that of the non-canonical Jain texts, which had best be called Jain Maharastri. The texts of the canon are undoubtedly of different ages, the oldest going back to near the time of Mahavira, while its later components, probably come down to near the time of Devarddhi.

According to Jain philosophy, matter, which consists of atoms is eternal, but may assume any form, such as earth, wind and so on. All material things are ultimately produced by combinations of atoms. Souls are of two kinds: those which are subject to mundane transmigration (*samsarin*) and those which are liberated (*mukta*). The latter will be embodied no more; they dwell in a state of perfection at the summit of the universe; being no more concerned with wordly affairs, they have reached *nirvana.*

The souls (*jiva*) with which the whole world is filled are different from matter; but being substances they are also eternal. Subtle matter coming into contact with a soul causes its embodiment: being then transformed into eight kinds of *karma* and thus forming as it were a subtle body, it clings to the soul in all its migrations. The theory of *karma* is the keystone of the Jain system. The highest goal consists in getting rid of all *karma* derived from past existences, and acquiring no new *karma*. One of the chief means to this end is the performance of asceticism (*tapas*). The Jain system differs from Buddhism in emphasizing asceticism to a much greater extent, even to the point of religious suicide; and in the total avoidance of taking life of any kind, such avoidance being described as the highest duty.

It is necessary for a Jain, in order to realize *nirvana,* to possess right faith, right knowledge, and right conduct. He is also required to observe the five vows, the first four of which are also acknowledged by the Brahmins and the Buddhists. These five consist of abstention from (i) killing, (2) lying, (3) stealing, (4) sexual intercourse, and (5) all attachment to worldly things, especially the owning of any possessions. Laymen were also to observe these vows, but only to the extent permitted by the conditions of their lives. Thus they were only obliged to refrain from intentionally killing animate beings, for otherwise they could not have gone about their business. Laymen were, in fact, more closely connected with the monastic order in Jainism than in early Buddhism. Jainism thus avoided fundamental changes, and has remained essentially unaltered for more than 2,000 years, while Buddhism underwent great transformations and disappeared from the land of its origin, its last remnants being expelled by Moslem attacks by about 1200 A.D.

Asceticism (*tapas*) is a very important institution in Jainism, for it not only prevents the formation of new *karma,* but extinguishes the old. Its austerities are of two kinds: external and internal. Fasting is the most conspicuous of the former. It has been developed by the Jains to a remarkable degree of elaboration. One of its forms is starving oneself to death. A form of external asceticism which Jainism has in common with Buddhism and Brahmanism is the practice of Yoga, or secluded meditation in certain recognized postures. Of all spiritual exercises the most important is contemplation (*dhyana*), or the concentration of the mind on a single object. Here there are four stages, in the last of which *karma* is annihilated. The soul then leaves the body and becomes liberated for ever. *Nirvana,* however, cannot be attained unless it is preceded by twelve years of self-mortification.

At the present day (1926) the Jain population of India amounts to 1,178,000. The smallness of this number *is* to be accounted for by the fact that Jainism is a religion of the upper classes, being no doubt too rigorous for the illiterate masses. But it is important in India owing to the wealth and education of its adherents. Their distinctive peculiarity of abstention from hurting any living thing excludes them from some professions, such as agriculture, and has forced them into commerce, especially money-lending. This explains both their wealth and their unpopularity.

The aggregate of their sacred books, or their canon, the Jains call their *Siddhanta* or their *Agama;* but only the Siddhanta of the Svetambara sect is as yet known to us. Besides the most important part of their canon, the twelve Angas, there are in the canon about thirty-six subordinate works, a dozen of which are called *Sutras*. The parts of the canon composed in verse are more archaic than the prose portions.

In the middle of the fifth century (454 A.D.) there was held a council at Vallabhi in Gujarat for the purpose of collecting and writing down the sacred texts. Though the age of these according to the tradition of the Svetambaras themselves is comparatively late, there are indications, in inscriptions and bas-reliefs of the first and second century A.D., of their authenticity going back to a much earlier date, especially as this probability is corroborated by the agreement with it, in many remarkable details, of the Buddhist tradition. The oldest elements of the canon may very well go back to the time of the first disciples of Mahavira, or at any rate to the council of Pataliputra, which was held according to tradition under the Maurya king Chandragupta at the end of the fourth century B.C., while the latest elements may be nearly as recent as the Council of Vallabhi.

In style we find that the canonical books show a mixture of prose and verse similar to that in the Pali Buddhist scriptures, but in doctrine much greater stress is laid on the principle of *ahimsa* and on rigorous asceticism, in the practice of which even religious suicide is recommended.

One of the Sutras, called the *Kalpa-sutra,* is the chief work supplying rules for the guidance of monks and nuns.

The first of four canonical texts called *Mula-sutras*

is the *Uttarajjhayana* (in Sanskrit *Uttaradhyayana*) *sutra*, a religious poem, which is one of the most valuable constituents of the canon. Its oldest parts consist of a series of maxims, parables, dialogues, and ballads of an ascetic type, which have parallels in Buddhist literature. It contains some fine epic dialogues and ballads, in which the ascetic ideal of the Jains is contrasted with that of the two highest castes (the Brahmin and the warrior) of Hinduism.

Many Commentaries

The non-canonical religious literature of the Jains consists partly of an immense number of commentaries, and partly of independent works on dogma, ethics, and monastic discipline, besides a very extensive body of poetical narrative. Between these two groups are didactic poems, legends of saints, and works on ecclesiastical history. The language in which this literature is written is partly the Prakrit called Jain Maharastri, and partly Sanskrit.

The chief value of the commentaries is that they preserve many old historical or semi-historical traditions, besides a large quantity of popular stories which the Jains, like the Buddhists, employed for illustrating their sermons. This Jain narrative literature has much in common with the Buddhist *Jatakas* and contains many elements which, reappearing in other forms of Indian and non-Indian literatures, are in fact the common property of world literature, Particularly rich in stories is the oldest commentary, consisting of nearly 600 verses, attributed to Bhadrabahu. The most important, however, of the commentaries are those of Santi Suri and Devendra Gani, the former of whom died in 1040 A.D. The Jains adopted a good deal of legendary matter from the Brahmin literature, such as the Krishna legend, and the epic story of the descent of the Ganges and the destruction of the 6o,coo sons of Sagara.

In later times the Jains made collections of stories, in which the tales were inserted one within the other and set in a general narrative framework, after the favourite Indian fashion. A rich fund of tales is the *Katha-kosa* or 'Treasury of Stories', written in bad Sanskrit, with verses in Prakrit. The well-known *Mahabharata* episode of *Nala and Damayanti* is one of the tales here introduced in a modified form.

A special type of poems meant for edification are the *caritras* and *prabandhas*. The former are biographies of ancient rulers and saints, while the latter are tales of monks and laymen of historical times. The monk Hemachandra was one of the most many-sided and prolific authors among the Jains, noted both as scholar and poet. He also composed works on such secular subjects as grammar, lexicography, poetics, and prosody. Born in 1089, he made Gujarat the chief seat of Jainism. His largest work was entitled *Trisasti-salaka-purusa-carita,* 'Life of the Sixty-three Best Men'. Much more important from the point of view of literary history is an appendix to this work entitled *Parisista-parvan,* or 'Supplementary Section', the stories in which are evidently derived from a popular source. Hemachandra translated them from Prakrit into Sanskrit.

A work of considerable importance for the textual criticism of one of the most famous poems of Sanskrit literature is the *Parsvabhyudaya,* a poetical biography of Parsvanatha, by Jinasena, composed about 800 A.D. In this poem the author incorporates the whole of the *Megha-duta,* a lyric of about 112 stanzas, by India's greatest poet in such a way as to borrow one or two lines in each stanza, which he completes in his own words.

The Jains also competed with the poets of other sects in the composition of religious lyrics. There are many such, called *stotras,* or 'hymns of praise', written in either Sanskrit or Prakrit and not altogether devoid of poetic merit. The oldest known poem of this kind is the *Uvasagga-harastotra,* a hymn of five stanzas addressed to Parsva and attributed to Bhadrabahu. A very old didactic poem in 540 Prakrit stanzas, intended to supply moral instruction for monks and laymen, is the *Uvaesa-mala* by Dharmadasa. The number of commentaries written on it, two of them dating from as early as the ninth century, attests its popularity.

One of the most important of the didactic poems of the Jainas is the *Yoga-sastra* of Hemachandra. It consists of a text in simple slokas and a commentary written in the artificial style of the Kavyas. The text contains a short sketch of the Jaina doctrine, while the commentary furnishes perhaps the clearest exposition that has ever been written of the whole system. The doctrine of *ahimsa* is strongly emphasized. Women, as is usual in this monkish poetry, are very pessimistically characterized. They are, for example, described as 'the torch on the road to the gate of hell, the root of all miseries, and the prime cause of discord'. Many of the verses in this poem on the transitoriness and vanity of human existence are up to the level of the best of the aphorisms of the Sanskrit poet Bhartrihari, as for instance: 'Fortune is fluctuating like the waves of the sea; the meeting of friends is like a dream; youth is like a blade of grass, whirled up by every gust of wind.'

The number of purely learned books on the Jaina religion is very great. One of the most prominent of the writers on philosophy is the voluminous Haribhadra, also known as an important commentator who flourished in the second half of the ninth century. He wrote the *Saddarsana-samuccaya*, 'Compendium of the Six Philosophical Systems'. Among these he includes Buddhism and Jainism. He also adds a short appendix on the materialist doctrine of Charvaka.

At a later period of Jainism the Digambara first, and afterwards the Svetambara sect, began to make use of Sanskrit not only for the purpose of writing on their own sectarian subjects. They also applied it in dealing with the secular scientific subjects of the Brahmins. They thus produced valuable works in Sanskrit on grammar and astronomy, and even in some departments of pure literature, which gained the approbation of their religious opponents. They also exercised an influence on the development of the languages of the south, in the literary cultivation of Kanarese, Tamil, and Telugu. The Jains thus occupy an important position in the history of the literature and civilization of India.

Jain Art

The Jain religion, like Buddhism, developed an art of its own, which was, however, evolved from the latter as its main source. Though Jainism as a religion was somewhat older than Buddhism, its art as a whole was much later. A few earlier examples of it have, indeed, survived, but it does not emerge in its main features till about 900 A.D. Its two leading types are simply modifications of the Dravidian and the Indo-Aryan styles of Hindu temple architecture. It is therefore only necessary here to point out its most distinctive features.

One of these, especially developed in the south, consisted in free-standing pillars almost invariably erected near the temples. They are the lineal descendants of the Buddhist detached columns bearing emblems or animal figures. These Jain pillars are nowhere so frequent or so elaborately carved as in the south. A variation of the free-standing columns are the commemorative towers (called *kirti-* or *jaya-stambha*) to be found in the north. One of these is a 'tower of fame' at Chittor in Rajasthan, dating from about 900 A.D. Another tower of this kind at the same place was finished in the year 1468 A.D. It is 133 feet high and consists of nine stories, the whole being covered with ornamental sculpture. Like the column of Trajan at Rome it is a 'pillar of victory', but in the words of Fergusson, the leading authority on Indian architecture, 'it is of infinitely better taste as an architectural object'.

The most distinctive feature of the Jain temple of the north is the porch erected in front of the cell containing the image of the Jain saint sitting cross-legged like the figure of Buddha. This porch consists of a circular dome resting on a group of eight pillars, every adjacent pair of which forms an arch by means of a connecting strut rising from a lower capital constructed some way below the top of the pillar. The strut thus gives additional support to the architrave resting on the summit of the column.

The dome is constructed by means of horizontal courses gradually approaching nearer by overlapping till the highest is closed with a slab at the top. The successive courses were doubtless originally octagonal, straight slabs being laid across at the angles. But the slabs came to be cut as segments of a circle, so as to form gradually narrowing rings of masonry till the highest closed the aperture at the top.

The great advantage of the horizontally constructed arch is the absence of a lateral thrust from which classical and Gothic buildings using the radiating arch suffer. Hence more slender and elegant pillars are possible in Indian architecture. Another result was the introduction of pendants in the centre of domes to a much greater extent than is found in any other style of building. The ornaments of the dome could here be introduced in concentric rings one above the other instead of on vertical ribs as in Roman and Gothic vaults. This allows far more variety without any lack of good taste, and has rendered some of the Jain domes more beautiful specimens of elaborate roofing than can be seen anywhere else.

5.

Epics and Classics

In the period of about a thousand years beginning with the Christian era the civilization of India, in its two main characteristics of the caste system and the belief in the transmigration of souls, was only a continuation of its preceding phase, but in the more widespread and intensified form that has held the Hindus in its grip down to the present day. There are also two other social institutions which developed during this period in India. The first, a custom dating from prehistoric times, which having hardly survived in the Vedic Age except in a symbolic funeral rite, revived, for some reason that is not quite clear, to such an extent that by about 600 A.D. it seems to have become universal, and would still be prevailing in India had it not been suppressed by the British Government in 1839.

This was the practice of the self-immolation of widows, on the death of their husbands, called *sati* ('virtuous woman') in Sanskrit. It may have been one of the economic effects of the caste system. The other, child-marriage, the growth of which was undoubtedly due to the increasing difficulty of securing suitable husbands belonging to the same caste as the daughter, is down to this day a characteristic of Hindu civilization. In 1921 the average age of marriage in Bengal was about twelve and a half for girls and rather under twenty for men.

The literary language of this period, Sanskrit, remained the same as in the preceding phase, for it had been stereotyped by the grammar of Panini, as we have seen, at least as early as the fourth century B.C. But though the growth of grammatical forms was thus arrested, the vocabulary of the language could not in a similar way be prevented from being modified. The same remark applies to style. Compared with the relatively advanced prose of the Brahmanas, Sanskrit literature, in which prose is rare, shows no progress in this later period, for it is still crude and clumsy. Its style, however, betrays some change. For it is much more artificial in consequence of the frequent use of long compounds and of the elaborate rules of poetics to which it is subjected. The bulk of Sanskrit literature, which is now poetry, especially the epics, is written in the Sloka metre, consisting of iambically-ending couplets of two lines of sixteen syllables. The other metres used, though mostly based on Vedic prototypes, are much more rigid in their construction.

The most striking difference between Vedic and Sanskrit literature is that the former is essentially religious, the latter, with few exceptions, profane.

Though the literature of this period is almost entirely secular, it reflects the religion of the period so fully that its character can be judged clearly enough. We can see that it has become very different from that of the Vedic Age. The three gods Brahma, Vishnu, and Siva are the leading deities of the pantheon, while the great gods of the Veda have sunk to a lower level, though Indra is still prominent as the chief deity of the warrior caste. New gods of a lesser order have come into being: such as Kubera, god of riches; Ganesa and Kartikeya, sons of Siva, respectively god of learning and of war; Lakshmi, goddess of beauty and of fortune; Durga, the terrible spouse of Siva; besides various serpent deities. While the outlook of the Vedas is joyous and optimistic, that of Sanskrit literature is tinged with melancholy and pessimism, which no doubt resulted from the now universally accepted doctrine of transmigration and *karma.* To this is most probably due the elaboration of Vishnu's Avatars, which in several cases appear in an animal form to save mankind from calamity.

Temple Culture

This main phase of Indian religion, usually called Hinduism, did not begin to express itself in the form of architecture and sculpture till Buddhism was already showing signs of decay. I have already indicated that the Buddhists were the first Indian builders and carvers in stone, though their religion was an offshoot of the much older Brahmin faith. It is only on Buddhist monuments that we find the earliest representations of Hindu deities, such as Indra and Lakshmi, from the second century B.C. onwards. The most ancient remains of independent Hindu religious art. architectural or sculptural, date only from several centuries after the beginning of our era. These considerations justify the presumption that Hindu religious art is derived from that of the Buddhists.

Such a presumption is borne out by the fact that the earliest extant Hindu temples are practically identical in form with the latest Buddhist specimens, differing from them only in having the image of a Hindu deity, instead of one of Buddha, placed in the shrine. Again, some of the sculptures in the earliest Hindu cave temples at Ellora are hardly distinguishable from those of the latest Buddhist specimens at that place. Though the whole surface of India is covered with Hindu temples, the vast majority are modern or comparatively modern. The oldest examples of Hindu architecture date from the sixth century A.D., and the best of them belong to the period between then and the thirteenth A.D.

An historical study of these monuments enables us to distinguish clearly between two styles, each of which exhibits a definite type from the beginning. The geographical distribution of these two types is interesting, for the southern or Dravidian style is found only within the tropics, or south of the twenty-third degree of northern latitude. The northern or Indo-Aryan style, on the other hand, appears practically only north of that line. Historical study, moreover, shows that the Hindu temples of both styles are developments of Buddhist prototypes. But the remarkable thing is that they are respectively the descendants of two entirely distinct classes of Buddhist building.

For it can be shown that the Hindu Dravidian temple has been evolved from the Buddhist monastery (*vihara*), while the Indo-Aryan type has been derived from the Buddhist *stupa*.

The Dravidian Style

The earliest representative of this type is a monolith temple at Mahabalipur, one of the seven Pagodas situated near the seashore, 35 miles south of Chennai.

It is hewn out of a single block of granite, dating from about 600 A.D. It is clearly Brahmanic in origin, as is shown by its sculptures as well as its inscriptions. It is also a model of a Buddhist monastery of four stories. The plan is square, the pyramidal tower representing the upper stories that contained the cells of the monks. A short way off is a structural shrine on the very brink of the sea.

The design of the regular Dravidian temple is a square base ornamented externally with pilasters and containing the cell that holds the image. Over the shrine rises the *sikhara,* a pyramidal tower always divided into stories, a division that never disappears in Dravidian temples. The tower is crowned with a small dome, either circular or octagonal in shape.

An early rock-cut temple of this kind on a grand scale is the Kailasa at Ellora, dedicated to Siva and dating from the eighth century A.D. A monolith on an enormous scale, it constitutes one of the wonders of the world. It is the culmination of the art of rock-cutting in India.

The later Dravidian temples from about 1000 A.D. stand in a large court surrounded by an enclosing wall. A special feature of this later type is the *gopuram,* or great gateway in the enclosing wall opposite the shrine. It has a storied tower resembling that of the shrine itself; but it is oblong, not square in shape, being twice as wide as it is deep. The best specimen of this later style is the temple at Tanjore, erected in 1035 A.D. The body consists of two stories about 80 feet high, while the pyramidal tower rises in eleven stories to a total height of 190 feet.

To each of the great Dravidian temples is attached a large tank for the religious ablutions of the worshippers. Such sacred tanks not within the temple area are frequent in southern India. These are called *teppa kulam* or raft tanks, across which at certain festivals the image of the god is taken on a raft to the shrine in the middle.

The Dravidian temple at Halebid, left unfinished in 1270 A.D., is one of the most remarkable monuments in India, being unmatched for the variety of detail and the exuberance of fancy in its ornamentation. There is perhaps no other temple in the world on the external carving of which such a marvellous amount of labour has been spent. Thus the lowest band of the frieze surrounding it contains a procession of about 3,000 elephants, no two of which exactly resemble one another.

The Indo-Aryan Style

The essential parts of the Indo-Aryan temple are the rectangular cell containing the image or symbol of the god, and a curvilinear steeple with vertical ribs by which it is surmounted. A porch is generally added in front of the doorway to the cell, but this is not essential.

This temple is well adapted to throw light on the origin of the Indo-Aryan style. Among the earliest of the northern type are some of the temples in the large group at Bhuvanesvar in Orissa, about 250 miles south of Calcutta. The older specimens seem to date from about 800 A.D., the series coming down to about 1300 A.D. The early form of this type is best represented by the Muktesvar shrine, which is called by Fergusson 'the gem of Orissan art'.

The origin of the Indo-Aryan spire has always been a puzzle to Eastern archaeologists. Thus Fergusson remarks: 'Neither the pyramid nor the tumulus affords any suggestion as to the origin of the form, nor the tower, either square or circular; nor does any form of civil or domestic architecture. It does not seem to be derived from any of these.' My own view that this spire has been evolved from the *stupa* cannot be elaborated here, because too many illustrations would be required to substantiate this theory.

A somewhat analogous evolution of the Buddhist *stupa* can be followed outside the bounds of India.

In the sculptural representation of the Hindu gods a remarkable innovation took place by the end of the first Christian century. Before that time they appeared in ordinary human form with two arms and one head in Buddhist sculpture. Literary and numismatic evidence further combine to indicate that down to the first century A.D. the gods were regarded as normally human in appearance.

Now the epic and classical Sanskrit literature after the beginning of our era describe the most important gods as having four arms and one of them four heads also. The same abnormality appears in early Hindu sculpture and remains a divine characteristic ever afterwards. This feature is most conspicuous in the three leading gods Brahma, Vishnu, and Siva. All three are represented with four arms, which hold the symbols distinctive of each. It is characteristic of Brahma to have four heads as well, for in Sanskrit literature he regularly bears the epithet 'four-faced'. It is of Siva, however, that we have the earliest concrete representation with four arms. The evidence of coins is here able to show, within the narrow limits of half a century, when this innovation arose. On a coin of the Graeco-Indian king Kadphises II, dating from about 50 A.D., Siva still appears as a two-armed deity; but in the reigns of his successors Kaniska, Huviska, and Vasudeva, four-armed gods become common beside two-armed examples, though the latter still continue to appear on coins till about 300 A.D.

We are thus justified in asserting that four-armed gods appear on coins from about 100 A.D. onwards, and that they had become an established type by 200 A.D. The first step in this innovation was the addition of two extra arms rising from the back of the shoulders. The four-armed type having once been established as a divine characteristic, the number of arms was gradually increased in Indian iconography. Thus eight-armed figures occur at least as early as 600 A.D. From the eighth century onwards Vishnu occasionally has eight arms, and some of his Avatars more than four. Siva also has eight and, as a dancing figure, sixteen arms. Though Hindu deities appear in the Buddhist sculptures of Gandhara in normal human form only, the influence of the many-headed Hindu type made itself felt in the later centuries of Mahayana Buddhist sculpture in India. The figures of the Bodhisattva Avalokitesvara are found with four or six arms, and even eleven heads. This feature followed Mahayanist Buddhism from India to other countries. Thus in Chinese Buddhist temples there appears a goddess with sixteen arms. This abnormality, however, does not seem ever to have extended to the figure of Buddha himself anywhere, probably because his image had early acquired a stereotyped character.

As the Indian gods originally lacked individuality, the early artist employed two means of differentiating them in sculpture. One was the addition of the *vahana,* or animal conveying the deity, as the elephant on which Indra rides. It is noteworthy that in all such cases the deity has only one head and only two arms; for the *vahana* serves to indicate both the divine nature and the identity of the deity. The second means of identification was the possession of many arms and heads, besides the holding of characteristic symbols. When the Indian artist found it necessary to omit the *vahana,* how was he to meet the difficulty when the two hands of the deity, being engaged in some kind of action or gesture, could not hold any symbol of identity? The addition of two extra arms might easily occur to him as an expedient, for this is obviously their purpose in Indian iconography.

The addition would, moreover, be no new idea, but merely the concrete expression of a Vedic figure of speech. Though the gods are normally regarded in the *Rigveda* as one-headed and two-armed, they are yet occasionally referred to figuratively as having an abnormal number of heads and arms. Thus Agni is said to be three-headed, obviously because the sacrificial fire burns on three altars; and Visvakarma is four-armed (*visvato-bahu* 'with an arm on every side'). The further divine characteristic of having four heads was added in the case of Brahma because his Vedic prototype Visvakarma is in the *Rigveda* described as 'facing in all directions' (*visvato-mukha*), and in post-Vedic literature as 'four-faced' (*catur-mukha*). Hence Brahma always appears in sculpture with four heads as well as four arms. The above considerations show that what is usually thought a monstrous feature of Hindu iconography is the natural outcome of an inherent necessity requiring the expression in sculpture of the divine character in general and the individuality in particular when the gods were represented in concrete form.

•

The products of Sanskrit literature, which are many-sided, may be divided into six groups: epic, lyric, dramatic, sententious or didactic, narrative, and scientific. The beginnings of all of them may be traced back to the preceding era of Sanskrit, but the earliest extant forms of at least the first five groups do not appear till after the commencement of our era. We have seen that as an actual fact the rich Pali literature of Buddhism arose in earlier centuries. The most ancient type of Sanskrit poetry in the shape of epic tales must have grown up in the preceding age also. Even in the *Rigveda* there are some hymns of a narrative character. Later, in the Brahmanas, several short legends appear, some of them partly metrical, as the story of Sunahsepa in the *Aitareya Brahmana.* The etymological work of Yaska, the *Nirukta,* written in Classical Sanskrit about 500 B.C., contains many prose tales; and the earliest extant collection of Vedic legends, the metrical *Brhaddevata,* must be nearly as old.

Epic Poetry

But the epics, in the form in which they have come down to us, date from after the beginning of the Christian era. Two classes of Sanskrit epic poetry must be distinguished. The first type, the language of which is simpler and conforms less to the strict rules of grammar, and the character of which is freer and of more spontaneous growth, is called *itihasa,* 'story', or *purana,* 'ancient legend'. The second, more regular in language and style, is termed *kavya,* 'poetical composition', representing a more artificial class, strictly subject to the rules of grammar and poetics, and the work of an individual poet. By far the most important as well as the oldest representative of the former class is the vast epic called *Mahabharata,* 'The Great Bharata Story'. The group of eighteen Puranas, or 'ancient legendary poems', are similar in style, but much later in date. The earliest representative of the artificial class is the other great Sanskrit epic, the *Ramayana*, 'The Adventures of Rama'. This type of epic reached its culmination under Kalidasa, about the beginning of the fifth century A.D.

The *Mahabharata* is a vast poem containing about 100,000 couplets, equivalent to about eight times the length of the Homeric poems. There is inscriptional evidence that it had attained that aggregate bulk by about 400 A.D. Its epic kernel, amounting to about one-fifth of the whole work, became so much overgrown with didactic matter that it could hardly be regarded as an epic at all, and has rather taken the place of a moral encyclopaedia in Indian literature.

It consists of eighteen books called *parvan,* to which is added as a supplement a nineteenth named the *Harivamsa.* For this immense congeries of epic and didactic matter tradition invented as the name of its author the designation Vyasa ('arranger').

Though three main editions of this great epic have been printed in India, at Calcutta, Bombay, and Madras respectively, no critical edition has yet appeared. Much uncertainty prevails as to the authenticity of the text because research has proved that it has undergone numerous changes, additions, and omissions. The readings of the Northern and the Southern manuscripts are widely divergent, and even within these two groups many differences appear. In the former group, again, at least five varying recensions have been distinguished, and in the southern group the divergences may prove to be still greater. The need of a critical edition is therefore evidently a pressing one. A considerable amount of preliminary work on the manuscript material has already been done, but whether a single text representing what the epic was about 400 A.D. can be produced is very doubtful. Inscriptions of the fifth century A.D. prove that the epic had the same length and character (i.e., was regarded as a *dharma-sastra* or 'compendium of ethics') in that century as it has now.

The epic nucleus of the *Mahabharata,* comprising about 20,000 couplets, relates how the dynasty of the Kurus was overthrown by the Pandus. The king of the Kurus in a gambling match cheats the Pandus, robs them of their kingdom, and banishes them for nineteen years. Finally a great battle lasting eighteen days takes place, when the Kurus are annihilated.

The main story is constantly interrupted by lengthy disquisitions, philosophical, religious, and moral, one of them extending to no fewer than 20,000 couplets. There are also several narrative episodes. One of the oldest and most beautiful of these is the story of Nala and Damayanti, two lovers who after enjoying several years of happy married life become separated by misfortune, but after many trying adventures are reunited in the end. The story contains numerous fine and pathetic passages. The emaciation and grief-stricken plight of Damayanti, as she wanders alone in the forest, is described as follows.. She appears

Like the young moon's slender crescent
Obscured by black clouds in the sky;
Like the lotus-flower uprooted,
All parched and withered by the sun;
Like the pallid night when Rahu
Has swallowed up the darkened moon.

The most famous of the philosophical episodes of the *Mahabharata* is the *Bhagavad-gita*, the 'Song of the Adorable One'. It is one of the most important works of Sanskrit literature. It is introduced at the point where the rival armies confront each other, ready to begin the great battle. Arjuna, the leader of the Pandus, hesitates to fight against his kinsmen. Krishna, who, being an incarnation of Vishnu, acts as his charioteer, puts an end to his scruples by showing that action, as the performance of one's duty in the world, is necessary, though in the end concentration on the supreme spirit is the only way to secure salvation. There is no evidence showing when this episode was incorporated in the epic, and who was its author.

The stages by which the epic developed from its original germ till it reached its final encyclopaedic form are matter of conjecture. It is, however, not improbable that it had assumed the character of a didactic compendium before the beginning of our era.

Essentially related to the *Mahabharata* is a group of legendary works called Puranas, of which there are eighteen. Deriving their subject-matter from the epics, the earliest of them cannot be older than the sixth century A.D. They are didactic religious sectarian manuals inculcating the worship chiefly of Vishnu, though some of them are associated with Siva. They deal mostly with cosmogony, the genealogy of the gods and patriarchs, and the history of royal dynasties. In that part of their matter which is peculiar to them they agree so closely that they must go back to some older work as a common source. The *Bhagavata Purana,* which contains about 18,000 slokas and derives its name from being a glorification of Bhagavata or Vishnu, has exercised a more powerful influence in India than any other poetical work of this type.

Beside the *Mahabharata* arose a second epic cycle, the *Ramayana,* which is not popular in character, but artificial both in the style of its descriptions and in the use of poetical figures. It is the forerunner of the later Court epics which are called Kavyas as a class. The *Ramayana* relates the adventures of Rama, son of Dasarath, king of Ayodhya. It consists of about 34,000 couplets and is divided into seven books. It has been shown to have originally consisted of five books (II-VI), in which some interpolated passages occur as well. Apart from interpolations this epic is the work of a single poet named Valmiki. The plot consists of two distinct elements, the first of which has every appearance of being based on historical tradition. The foundation of the second is mythological; for it is full of marvellous and fantastic incidents, and the main figures are traceable in Vedic literature.

The original epic, as composed by the poet Valmiki, was transformed, by the addition of the first and last books, into a poem glorifying Vishnu, of whom Rama is represented as an incarnation. This identification has turned the hero of the epic into an object of lasting worship among, the Hindus, and has secured to the *Ramayana* a greater popularity in India than probably any other product of Sanskrit literature. Its story has furnished the subject of many other Sanskrit poems as well as plays. It has also been translated into many Indian vernaculars. The most important adaptation is the Hindi version of Tulasi Das (1532-1633), the greatest poet of medieval Hindustan; for it is a kind of bible to nearly crores of people of northern India.

As the *Mahabharata* was the chief source of the Puranas, so the *Ramayana* became the model of a number of Court epics almost all of which belong to the period between 400 and 1100 A.D. From the direct evidence of a dated inscription and of the poet Bana, who lived under King Harshavardhan, the ruler of the whole of northern India from 606 to 648 A.D., we know that Kalidasa and other famous classical poets flourished before 600 A.D. There is, moreover, some valuable literary and epigraphical evidence that this type of poetry originated not later than about 200 B.C. and continued to be cultivated during the succeeding centuries. The earliest preserved of the post-Christian Kavyas is the *Buddha-carita,* 'Life of Buddha', by Asvaghosha, one of the oldest Buddhist works in Sanskrit, belonging to the end of the second century A.D.

As to Kalidasa, the most famous poet of India, we have good reason to believe that he flourished in the first half of the fifth century. His knowledge of Greek astronomy in any case indicates that he cannot have lived earlier than 300 A.D. His two Court epics are the *Raghuvamsa,* 'The Race of Raghu', and the *Kumara-sambhava*, 'The Birth of the War-god'. The former describes the life of Rama, besides giving an account of his forefathers and successors. It contains much genuine poetry. The style, though still comparatively simple, is in many passages too artificial for the western taste. As nearly one-half of the *Kumara-sambhava* is concerned with the courtship and wedding of the god Siva and the goddess Parvati, the parents of the youthful divinity, description is its prevailing characteristic. Both in originality of treatment and beauty of style and thought, these two epics are superior to later works of this type.

The subjects of these later poems are derived from

the two great epics. Intermingled with lyric, erotic, and didactic elements, they become more artificial the further they are removed from Kalidasa's time.

The *Kiratarjuniya.* by Bharavi, who lived not later than the sixth century A.D., is a poem describing a combat between Siva, disguised as a *Kirata* or mountaineer, and Arjuna. One of its cantos includes a number of stanzas illustrating various kinds of verbal tricks. One stanza, for instance, contains no consonant but *n,* except a single *t* at the end.

Another artificial epic, the *Bhatti-kavya,* ascribed to the poet and grammarian Bhartrihari, who died in 651 A.D., relates the story of Rama, with the sole object of illustrating the forms of Sanskrit grammar.

The *Sisupala-vadha,* or 'Death of Sisupala', by the poet Magha, dates from the second half of the seventh century. One of its cantos teems with metrical puzzles, some of a highly complex character. Thus one stanza read backwards is identical with the preceding one read in the ordinary way. This work, nevertheless, does not lack poetical beauties and striking thoughts.

The *Nalodaya,* or 'Rise of Nala', dealing with a well-known episode of the *Mahabharata,* describes the restoration to power of King Nala. The chief aim of the author is to display his skill in manipulating artificial metres and elaborate tricks of style. The exiguous narrative running through the poem is interrupted by long descriptions and lyrical effusions. The most noteworthy feature of this work is the introduction of rhyme, which is employed not only at the end, but in the middle of metrical lines. This is an innovation in Sanskrit poetry shared by the *Gita-govinda* and the *Moha-mudgara.* This novel feature is probably due to Prakrit influence; for hyme was an essential element of versification in Prakrit, as it is of modern Indian vernaculars.

The culmination of artificial ingenuity is the *Raghava-pandaviya,* an epic composed about 800 A.D. by a poet named Kaviraja. By the use of ambiguous words and phrases the story of the *Ramayana* and that of the *Mahabharata* are here related at one and the same time.

Lyrical Poetry

This branch of Sanskrit literature must have arisen in the early centuries of our era, for a specimen of its fully developed form has been preserved from the early fifth century in Kalidasa's *Meghaduta,* or 'Cloud Messenger'. It consists of some 113 stanzas of four lines and is composed in a metre of seventeen syllables to the line called *manda-kranta.* ('advancing slowly'). The theme is a message which an exile in central India sends by a cloud to his wife in the Himalayas. The sight of a dark cloud moving northward at the approach of the rainy season fills him with yearning and suggests the thought of entrusting to this aerial envoy a message of hope to his wife in his mountain home. In the first half of the poem the exile delineates with much power and charm the various scenes to be traversed by the cloud on its northward course. In the second half he describes the beauties of his home on mount Kailasa, and then the loveliness, the occupations, and the grief of his wife. The following is a stanza of his message:

In creepers I discern thy form; in eyes of startled hinds thy glances;
And in the moon thy lovely face; in peacock's plumes thy shining tresses;

The sportive frown upon thy brow in flowing
waters' tiny ripples:
But never in one place combined can I, alas! behold
thy likeness.

But looking forward to their reunion he adds;

And then we will our heart's desire, grown more
intense by separation,
Enjoy in nights all glorious and bright with full-
orbed autumn moonlight.

There is another beautiful lyrical poem entitled *Rtu-samhara,* or 'Cycle of the Seasons', consisting of 153 stanzas divided into six cantos and composed in various metres. It is a highly poetical description of the six seasons into which the Indian year is divided by Sanskrit poets. By introducing love-scenes the author skilfully combines the expression of human emotions with glowing accounts of the beauties of nature. Perhaps no other Sanskrit poem manifests such strikingly deep sympathy with the physical world, keen powers of observation, and skill in depicting an Indian landscape in vivid colours. This poem is attributed to Kalidasa, and, judged by its merits, such an ascription might very well be correct. The poem also seems to belong to the age of Kalidasa. But the fact that the *Rtusamhara* is never quoted in the Sanskrit works on poetics weighs heavily against its attribution to Kalidasa.

There are two other lyrics, the *Caura-pancasika* and the *Ghata-karpara,* comprising respectively fifty and twenty-two stanzas, but otherwise much of this type of literature is found in the dramas. The greater part of Sanskrit lyrical poetry appears in the form of single stanzas in which an amatory situation or sentiment is drawn with a few strokes and often by a master hand. Several poets composed collections of these miniature lyrics, which frequently display great wealth of illustration and depth of feeling. The most distinguished poet of this type is Bhartrihari, who lived in the first half of the seventh century A.D. His *Sringara-sataka,* or 'Hundred Stanzas of Love', shows him, in graceful and meditative verse, to be fully susceptible to the charms of women and well acquainted with the arts by which they captivate the hearts of men. The most important collection of love-lyrics is the *Amaru-sataka,* or 'Hundred Stanzas of Amaru'. The author is a master in the art of painting lovers in all their moods—bliss and dejection, anger and devotion. His main strength perhaps lies in depicting the various stages of estrangement and reconciliation. The love that Amaru, like other Indian lyrists, delineates is undoubtedly of the sensual type, not the romantic and ideal. Delicacy of feeling and refinement of thought are, however, not lacking in this poetry. The plant and animal world, which here plays an important part, is treated with much charm.

The following stanza from Bhartrihari may serve as an. example of Indian lyric poetry:

Beside the lamp, the flaming hearth,
In light of sun or moon and stars,
Without my loved one's lustrous eyes
This world is wholly dark to me.

The transition from pure lyric to pure drama is represented in form, though not chronologically (for it dates from the twelfth century A.D.), by the *Gita-govinda,* or 'Cowherd in Song'. It is the earliest literary specimen of a primitive type of play that still survives in Bengal, and must have preceded the developed drama. There is no dialogue in the proper sense, for each of the three characters merely engages in a kind of lyrical monologue, to which one of the other two is generally supposed to listen. The subject is the love of Krishna for the beautiful Radha, their estrangement, and final reconciliation. It is a highly artificial poem in which its author Jayadeva shows great perfection of form by combining grace of diction with ease in handling the most intricate metres. He makes much use of alliteration and very complex rimes, adapting, with unsurpassable skill, the most varied and melodious measures to the expression of exuberant erotic emotions. This poem brings us to the regular Sanskrit drama, which is a combination of lyric stanzas and prose dialogue.

The Drama

The origin of the acted drama of India is wrapped in obscurity. Even as early as the *Rigveda,* dialogue is the form of some of its hymns. But between these and the actual Sanskrit plays that have come to us, to none of which can an earlier date than 300 A.D. be assigned, the gap is enormous. Nor is there any direct evidence of any connexion between the two. The indirect testimony of language, however, furnishes a clue as to the source of the Sanskrit drama. The Sanskrit words for 'actor' and 'play' are *nata* and *nataka* respectively. These are Prakrit derivatives of the root *nat,* the vernacular form of the Sanskrit *nrt*, 'to dance', and familiar to English ears in the guise of 'nautch', as the performance of professional female dancers in India.

These names, as vernacular words and because of their meanings, suggest that the Indian drama was popular in origin, and that some rude form of pantomime was its starting-point. Panini, in the fourth century B.C., speaks of *natas,* or 'dancers', and mentions *nata-sutras,* or 'handbooks for dancers'. The contents were later utilized by Bharata in a larger treatise entitled *Natya-sastra,* or 'Principles of the Dramatic Art', the age of which cannot be fixed with certainty, but which may possibly date from as early as 300 B.C. It deals with all that concerns the drama: singing, music, dancing, metre, the use of different dialects, and so on. All later works on the drama are based on Bharata's treatise. The most important of these is the *Dasa-rupa,* or 'The Ten Kinds (of drama)', which deals with drama in the narrow sense and was composed by Dhananjaya in the tenth century A.D.

As regards the ultimate source of the Indian drama, various scholars are inclined to find it in several hymns of the *Rigveda,* which, being unconnected with the ritual, are of a narrative character and sometimes appear in the form of a dialogue. This inference is *a priori* possible, but there is no evidence to prove that such a development actually took place. Other scholars trace the origin of the Indian drama to the influence of the Greeks. They argue that at the time of Alexander the Great's invasion of India (326 B.C.) numerous Greek artists accompanied his expedition, and that subsequently the frontier countries of India were ruled by Greek kings, who must have supported Greek theatres. But there are no ascertained facts to substantiate this theory; nor is it necessary to explain the existence of the Indian drama in this way. For its whole development can be satisfactorily accounted for by Indian antecedents.

Indian plays are throughout not very dramatic in style. The delineation of character is weak, being concerned rather with types than with human beings of real flesh and blood. The development of the story often depends on an external accident such as a curse, and the plot itself is often nothing more than a loosely connected series of pictures or epic scenes. The Greek theory is chiefly based on the *Mrcchakatika*; but the earliest Indian plays that have survived are of quite a different kind, and have no resemblance to the Greek drama. It is true that one of the names of the curtain (*yavanika*, i.e., 'Ionian') is the 'Greek (appliance)'; but it is more likely that the whole stage or the drama itself should have been designated by 'Greek', if the latter had been introduced from a foreign country. Not only does the Greek theory err in overlooking the earliest Indian dramatic productions, but the chief class of the Indian drama, called *nataka,* bears no similarity to the Greek mime.

The most likely explanation is that the Indian drama derives its origin from scenes of an histrionic and a popular character which are imitated in the Vedic ritual; as when a Brahmin buys Soma from a Sudra, who is then driven out with sticks. Such scenes of horseplay would be accompanied by dance, song, and music, which are designated as the most important elements of the dramatic art (*natya*). It is also noteworthy that the ordinary words for 'actor', 'play', and 'dramatic art' are, as has already been said, derived from the vernacular root *nat,* 'to dance'. The mimic dance becomes drama as soon as words are added. We know from the ritual Vedic texts that dance, music, and song were employed at sacrifices and religious festivals. We are informed that on such occasions the *natas* celebrated the performance in song; that they occasionally composed the accompanying words and sometimes produced much laughter. This points to the existence of actual mimes.

The use in this way of popular artists naturally led to their art being systematically treated in handbooks. Some light is further shed on the development of the drama by a number of modern plays and by the so-called *yatras,* which represent a mythological subject and especially the Krishna legend. Several features of the regular plays indicate that a popular pantomime was a preliminary aspect of the Indian drama: the dialogue between the stage-manager and actress at the beginning of the play; the employment of different dialects; the mixture of prose and lyrics; the combination of dance and music; the simplicity of the stage; and the retention of the jester (*vidusaka*). The great antiquity of these Indian phenomena excludes a Greek origin. It was at one time believed by Sanskrit scholars that Patanjali (second century B.C.) in his *Mahabhasya,* a commentary on Panini's grammar, mentions the existence of an actual Indian drama, but as the passage in which this was supposed to be stated has been proved to be mistranslated, it has no chronological value in this question.

The rise of the Indian drama is thus most probably due to the coalescence of recited epic legend with ancient pantomimic art. But we know nothing of the history of the actual drama till we come across it fully developed about 100 A.D. It probably arose in the land of the Surasenas at Mathura, their capital. We have no reason to suppose that it came into being more than a century before the time of Asvaghosha.

The main characteristics of the Sanskrit drama are these. Lyrical stanzas, composed in various metres, interchange with prose dialogue. In *Sakuntala* the former comprise about one-half of the whole play. The prose of the dialogue is often very commonplace, serving only to introduce the lofty sentiment of the following lyric. Sanskrit plays consequently appear deficient in action when compared with European dramas. A further peculiarity is that they employ different dialects according to the social position of the speakers. Sanskrit is used by heroes, kings, Brahmins, and men of rank. Prakrit (*Sauraseni, Maharastri, Magadhi*) is spoken not only by women, but by men of the lower orders.

Tragedy is unknown on the Indian stage. No deeply tragical incident, such as death, may take place on it, nor is there ever a sad ending. Hence terror, pity, and grief are always assuaged by the happy conclusion of the story. The plot is commonly derived from history or epic legend. The main theme of most Indian plays is love. The hero, who is usually a king and already married to one or more wives, falls in love at first sight with some beautiful girl. The heroine reciprocates his love, but conceals her passion. The ensuing doubts and delays plunge both into a state of melancholy and despair. The depressing effect produced by their doleful plight is counteracted by the lively activity of the heroine's confidantes and especially of the jester (*vidusaka*), who usually plays a prominent part as the constant companion of the hero. Finally, all ends happily.

The structure of a Sanskrit play is this. It is divided into acts which vary in number according to its character. The act is divided into scenes, which are marked off by the entrance of one character and the exit of another. The stage is never left vacant, and the locality remains the same till the end of the act. The play usually opens with a prologue on the stage, where the manager and one or two of the actors converse about the piece that is to follow. Goethe adopted this feature from Kalidasa's *Sakuntala* in his *Faust*.

A necessary part of the stage arrangement was a curtain, divided in the middle, which did not separate the audience from the stage, but formed its background. Behind the curtain was the tiring room, whence the actors entered the stage. The scenery and decorations being very simple, much was left to the imagination of the spectator, as in the Shakespearian drama. Owing to intercourse between heaven arid earth being frequently represented, there was, however, probably some kind of contrivance suggesting an aerial car, in which the impression of motion and speed would be produced by the gestures of the actors.

We do not know when the first actual play was written in India. But the earliest dramatic author of whose work anything has survived is Asvaghosha, the famous Buddhist teacher of the Mahayana school. He wrote at least one drama, the *Sariputra-prakarana*. It is divided into nine acts, its subject being the conversion of the two chief pupils of Buddha, Sariputra and Maudgalyayana. Manuscript fragments of this drama, which go back to Kusana times (*c.* 100 A.D.), have been found at Turfan in Central Asia, and have been edited. Certain features, such as the figure of the *vidusaka* or jester, indicate that the author had predecessors. It does not, however, seem likely that the drama had a long history before Asvaghosha. As he was, according to tradition, a teacher of King Kanishka (125), Asvaghosha has been assigned to the second century A.D.

Fragments of two other Buddhist dramas have been found in the same region of Chinese Turkistan and appear on palaeographic grounds to belong to the same period; but there is no evidence showing who wrote them. A Sanskrit Buddhist work, the *Avadana-sataka,* which was translated into Chinese in the third century A.D., mentions a Buddhist drama acted by South Indian players before the king of Sobhavati. There thus seems good reason to believe that by 200 A.D. the Sanskrit drama was an established institution.

The best surviving specimens of the Sanskrit drama produced between *c.* 200 and 800 A.D. number nearly a dozen. The greatest playwright was Kalidasa, who cannot have lived earlier than about 400 A.D. He had a famous predecessor named Bhasa, whose works were, however, till recently regarded as lost long ago. The evidence for the existence of this ancient poet is the following. Kalidasa (*c.* 400 A.D.) in his drama *Malavikagnimitra* mentions Bhasa as a poet whose fame he cannot rival. Bana, in the introduction to his historical romance *Harsa-carita* (*c.* 620 A.D.), states that Bhasa obtained fame by plays *{nataka}* in the beginning of which the *sutradhara,* or stage manager, appeared. A verse of Rajasekhara (*c.* 1000 A.D.) mentions a *Svapna-vasavadatta,* or 'Dream-Vasavadatta', as Bhasa's work, which, being thrown into the fire as a test of its merit, stood the test successfully. In the *Gaudavaho,* or 'Death of Garuda', by the Prakrit poet Vakpatiraja (*c.* 750 A.D.), Bhasa receives the designation *jalana-mitta,* or 'friend of conflagration', perhaps in allusion to the same incident. We have thus four references in Sanskrit and Prakrit literature up to 1000 A.D. proving the existence of Bhasa as an eminent dramatic poet. There also occur in his commentary, on a rhetorical work entitled *Dhvanyaloka,* by Abhinavagupta (*c.* 1000 A.D.) and in the Sanskrit anthologies of later centuries about a dozen quotations there attributed to Bhasa.

In 1912 there were published in southern Malabar, at Trivandrum, thirteen Sanskrit plays that were by the editor, followed by most Sanskrit scholars, identified with the long lost works of Bhasa. The sole basis of this far-reaching identification is that, although all these plays are anonymous, the title of a single one of them, *Svapna-nataka* (in one manuscript entitled *Svapna-vasavadatta*), may be the same as that of the only play, *Svapna-vasavadatta,* twice mentioned by ancient authorities as the work of Bhasa. The uncertainty as to the same play being meant by the divergent titles is increased by the fact that a verse quoted by Abhinavagupta on the *Dhvanyaloka* as occurring in the *Svapna-vasavadatta.* is not to be found in the *Svapna-nataka.* The supposed identity of these two titles is the only clue available as to the authorship of the *Svapna-nataka.* For, contrary to the general practice of Sanskrit dramas, the *Svapna-nataka* does not name its author. Thus even this support for the identification of the Trivandrum play with the ancient *Svapna-vasavadatta* of the real Bhasa is wanting.

The very dubious identification of the Trivandrum *Svapna-nataka* with the *Svapna-vasavadatta* of the ancient poet Bhasa, on the strength of the possible identity of their titles, but without the support of any corroborative evidence, is made the basis of the much more far-reaching and uncertain conclusion that the other twelve recently published plays are, owing to their great similarity of style and the possession of many passages in common, not only the production of one and the same poet, but that that poet is Bhasa. Not only are all these plays anonymous, but we do not even know any of the titles of the plays of the ancient Bhasa except only *Svapna-vasavadatta*. Now the similarity in style of these thirteen plays may very well be due to the peculiarities and exigencies of the stage in Malabar, where alone these plays are known and acted. No attempt at investigation in this direction has yet been made, at least by any of the western supporters of this hypothesis. Again, many of the views expressed as to the relative merits of these plays are purely subjective, and can have no decisive cogency in regard to facts.

No confirmation of the Bhasa hypothesis is to be derived from the quotations attributed to Bhasa in rhetorical works and anthologies. For none of the fourteen quotations there ascribed to Bhasa occur either in the *Svapna-nataka* or in any of the other twelve plays; nor have any of the verses occurring in the Trivandrum plays been found in rhetorical works and anthologies even ascribed to some other author than Bhasa.

The diction of these plays shows familiarity with the style of the Puranas, and contains far more grammatical irregularities than the classical Sanskrit dramas do.

On the definite assumption, which, however, has no sound basis, that these thirteen Trivandrum plays are the work of the one author Bhasa, attempts have been made to fix their approximate date, chiefly on the evidence of the Prakrit appearing in the prose passages. By a comparison of this Prakrit with that of Asvaghosha and Kalidasa, one of the conclusions arrived at is that Bhasa comes chronologically midway between these two, and therefore belongs to the third century A.D. Though this, of course, cannot prove anything as to the individual authorship of the plays, it could show that they were composed at the time when Bhasa probably lived, and that consequently he might have been the author of some of them.

But here it seems necessary to investigate the position of Prakrit in Malabar very carefully before it can be made the basis of decisive chronological conclusions. For here it was an exotic, the natural development of which, on its transplantation to the entirely alien linguistic area of a Dravidian country, at once became arrested, while in its home in northern India it would be liable to regular change as the literary form of a spoken vernacular. Estimates of the age of these plays on the evidence of their Prakrit should thus be undertaken with great caution. As it is, the calculation of their age, whether based on the character of their Prakrit or on other considerations, varies very greatly: that of Western scholars between the second and seventh century A.D., that of Indian scholars between the fifth century B.C. and the tenth A.D.

The above summary criticisms probably suffice to show that the attribution of these thirteen plays, or even of one of them, to Bhasa is subject to much doubt at every point. Far more cogent evidence than is yet available is necessary to prove that any one of the lost plays of Bhasa has survived to the present day. The verdict, in my view, cannot as yet be any other than 'not proven'. A certain conclusion based on data no one of which is more than a possibility is inadmissible. The difficulties of this problem may perhaps be successfully grappled with by minutely investigating the history of the Sanskrit drama in Malabar.

The two greatest Sanskrit playwrights were Kalidasa and Bhavabhuti. The former of these is the more eminent, famous as an epic and a lyric poet as well. He wrote three dramas, *Sakuntala*, *Vikramorvasi*, and *Malavikagnimitra*. The first two are the best specimens of the romantic drama of India. They represent the love adventures of two famous kings of ancient days, dealing with matters heroic and divine, far removed from the realities of everyday life. The third is a palace and harem drama of contemporary love and intrigue.

In *Sakuntala* the poet presents the romance of King Dushyanta and the daughter of a celestial nymph. Engaged in the chase, the king sees Sakuntala, whom he falls in love with and marries. After his return home, Sakuntala is sent by her guardian, the hermit Kanva, to her husband, who, however, in consequence of the curse of an angry sage, fails to recognize her. A long separation ensues, till finally the two are reunited through the agency of a ring which, having been formerly given by the king to his wife and having later been swallowed by a fish, has been recovered by fishermen. Its lack of action renders *Sakuntala*, like almost all Sanskrit dramas, defective as a stage play. But it has many beauties. The richness of his creative fancy, and his skill in expressing tender sentiment and sympathy with nature, gives Kalidasa a high place among the world's dramatic poets. The following few lines may serve as a specimen. They are uttered by the old sage Kanva when his ward Sakuntala is about to leave her home, the forest hermitage, to rejoin her husband:

> *My heart is touched with sadness when I think*
> *'Sakuntala must leave to-day; my throat*
> *Is choked with flow of tears repressed; mine eyes*
> *Grow dim with pensiveness; but if the grief*
> *Of this old forest hermit is so great,*

How keen must be the pang a father feels
When freshly parted from a cherished child!

Then, turning to the trees of the grove to give Sakuntala a sign of farewell, he adds:

The trees, the kinsmen of her forest home,
Now to Sakuntala give leave to go:
They with the Kokila's melodious cry
Their answer make.

Then voices in the air utter the following good wishes as she departs:

Thy journey be auspicious; may the breeze,
Gentle and soothing, fan thy cheek; may lakes
All bright with lily cups delight thine eye;
The sunbeams' heat be cooled by shady trees;
The.dust beneath thy feet the pollen be of lotuses.

Kalidasa also shows moderation and sense of proportion, somewhat rare qualities in Indian literature. The perfections of *Sakuntala* earned the highest praise from so eminent a critic as Goethe. To its widespread popularity in India is probably due to the fact that this drama exists in four recensions, none of which can be said to represent the original text more closely than any of the others. *Vikramorvasi*, or 'Urvasi (won) by Valour', deals with the romance of King Pururavas and the nymph Urvasi, the earliest form of which occurs in the *Rigveda*, far more than a thousand years before. Urvasi is parted from her lover as the result of his being summoned before the throne of the god Indra; but, after undergoing many trials caused by separation, the lovers are re-united in consequence of Indra's favour, which Pururavas gains by his services against the demons.

Malavikagnimitra, though inferior to the other two dramas in poetic merit, has many beauties of its own. Based on the ordinary palace life of Indian princes, it affords a good picture of the social conditions of the time. Its theme is the loves of King Agnimitra, who reigned at Vidisa (Bhilsa) in the second century B.C., and of Malavika, one of the attendants of the queen. As the heroine finally turns out to be a princess by birth and there is therefore no longer any impediment to her union with the king, all ends happily.

A drama entitled *Mrcchakatika,* or 'The Little Clay Cart', is attributed to a king named Sudraka, whose date it seems impossible to determine, but is probably not far removed from that of Kalidasa. An incomplete form of it, consisting of its first four acts, but without introductory and concluding verses, has been preserved under the title of *Carudatta,* as one of the thirteen plays published in the Trivandrum Sanskrit Series, and regarded by the adherents of the Bhasa hypothesis as the work of Bhasa. It looks like another recension of the *Mrcchakatika* adapted for performance on the Malabar stage. The *Mrcchakatika* is pre-eminent among Indian plays for the distinctively dramatic qualities of vigour, life, and action, as well as skill in the delineation of character. The scene is laid in the city of Ujjain, and is crowded with characters. The hero is Charudatta, a Brahmin merchant reduced to poverty by excessive liberality, and the heroine Vasantasena, a rich courtesan, who loves and ultimately marries Charudatta. The play abounds with comic situations diversified with many serious scenes.

Two plays are attributed to King Sriharsha, whom

we have already come across as Harshavardhana of Kanauj (606-48 A.D.). One of these is *Ratnavali,* or 'The Pearl Necklace', which reflects the court life of the age, and somewhat resembles the *Malavikagnimitra.* of Kalidasa. It represents the love-story of Udayana, king of Vatsa, and of Sagarika, an attendant of his queen Vasavadatta. The heroine ultimately turns out to be Ratnavali, princess of Ceylon, who has found her way to Udayana's court after suffering shipwreck. Forming a sequel to the popular love-story of Vasavadatta, this drama is an agreeable work with well-drawn characters and many poetical beauties. Of the; latter, the following passage on the approach of night may serve as an illustration:

Our minds intent upon the festival,
We saw not that the twilight passed away:
Behold, the east proclaims the lord of night
Still hidden by the hill where he will rise,
Even as a maiden by her pallid face
Reveals that in her heart a lover dwells.

Similar is the plot of another play by Sriharsha, entitled *Priyadarsika,* after a princess who was the daughter of the king of Anga, and was destined for king Udayana. By the vicissitudes of war she becomes an attendant, under the name of Aranyika, in the harem of the king, who sees and falls in love with her. Queen Vasavadatta, becoming suspicious, has her locked up. But on finding out that she is a princess of Anga she recognizes her as Priyadarsika, releases her, and arranges to have her married to Udayana. Sriharsha's third play is the *Nagananda,* the plot of which is derived from the legendary store of the *Brihatkatha*. It is a sensational piece of considerable merit, with a Buddhist colouring.

The second greatest Indian dramatist, the authenticity of whose plays is undoubted, Bhavabhuti, lived in the first half of the eighth century. He was a Brahmin of Vidarbha. He was well acquainted with the city of Ujjain, but spent part of his life under the patronage of King Yasovannan of Kanauj. Three of his plays, all abounding in poetical beauties, have come down to us. They differ from the works of the earlier dramatists in various points. Owing to Bhavabhuti's deeply serious temperament, the comic element is almost entirely lacking, and the jester does not appear in his plays. He prefers to depict the grand and sublime rather than the delicate and mild aspects of nature. He also displays skill in expressing depth and force of passion, as well as tender and noble sentiment. The most popular of his plays is the *Malati-madhava.* Ujjain is the scene, and the plot is concerned with the love-story of Malati, daughter of a minister of the country, and Madhava, a young scholar studying in the city. They fall in love, and in spite of the king's determination that the heroine shall marry his favourite, whom she detests, the lovers succeed in being finally united.

The other two plays deal with the fortunes of Rama, but, owing to lack of action, they have the character of dramatic poems rather than of dramas. The earlier part of Rama's career is presented in the *Mahavira-carita*, or 'Adventures of the Great Hero'. The *Uttara-Ramacarita,* or 'Later Adventures of Rama', contains some passages of more genuine pathos than perhaps any other Indian drama.

Though his date cannot be fixed with certainty, the dramatist Bhatta-Narayana must have lived before 800 A.D., as he is quoted by Vamana, the writer on poetics, in the eighth century. A well-known play by him is the

Venisamhara, or 'Binding of the Braid of Hair', the main incident of which is derived from the *Mahabharata.* Its popularity in India is chiefly due to its partiality for the cult of Krishna. Probably not later than 800 A.D. was composed a play of a unique type, Visakhadatta's *Mudraraksasa,* or 'Rakshasa and the Seal'. Love does not enter into the plot, for it is entirely a political piece, full of life, action, and sustained interest. The plot is concerned with the endeavour of the Brahmin Chanakya, the minister of Chandragupta, to win over to his master's cause the noble Rakshasa, formerly minister of a king deposed by Chandragupta in 315 B.C.

About 900 A.D. lived, during the reigns of the rulers of Kanauj, Mahendrapala and his successor Mahipala, the dramatist Rajasekhara, noted for his command of Sanskrit and Prakrit, as well as his knowledge of the spoken vernaculars. He uses many rare words and provincialisms. He also shows great skill in the employment of artificial metres. Now and then he avails himself of rhyme, which he borrowed from popular poetry. He is particularly fond of using proverbial phrases.

Two of his dramas deal with epic subjects. One is the *Balaramayana,* or 'Ramayana for Boys', which treats at excessive length the story of the whole *Ramayana* in ten acts. The *Balabharata,* or 'Mahabharata for Boys', has been left uncompleted or, with the exception of the first two acts, has been lost. These deal with the marriage of Draupadi and with the gambling scene of the epic in which she is dragged by her hair before the assembly by one of the Kauravas.

Another of Rajasekhara's plays, the *Viddhasalabhanjika,* or 'The Statue', is not lacking in comic situations, for which the fact that the heroine is a girl disguised as a boy affords abundant opportunities.

His *Karpura-manjari* is one of the best comedies in Indian literature. It is the only extant well-known drama entirely composed in Prakrit. Rajasekhara apparently wanted to show that, after making his name as a Sanskrit poet, he was able to deal with the most difficult metres in Prakrit quite as well as in Sanskrit. Rajasekhara's plays deserve to be studied for the correctness of their diction and the smoothness of their verses both in Sanskrit and Prakrit, as well as for the proverbial sayings with which they abound and the allusions which they contain to the customs prevailing in his day. He is, however, not a great poet, for he lacks taste and originality.

The *Hanuman-nataka,* or 'Play of Hanuman', a rambling piece of little merit, represents the adventures of Rama in so far as they are connected with his ally, the monkey king. It is also known by the title *Mahanataka*, 'The Great Drama'. It must have been written before 850 A.D., as it is quoted by Anandavardhana, the writer on poetics, in his *Dhvanydloka* (*c.* 850 A.D.). It is known in two rather widely divergent recensions, one of which; the western, ascribed to Damodara Misra, contains 581 stanzas in fourteen acts, while the other, that of Bengal, attributed to Madhusudana, contains 730 stanzas in nine acts. The text abounds in interpolations. It can hardly be regarded as a drama, but rather comes half-way between an epic and a dramatic poem. It has no *vidusaka,* nor does it contain any Prakrit speeches.

One of the most remarkable products of Indian literature, which dates from *c.* 1100 A.D., is the *Prabodha-candrodaya,* or 'Rise of the Moon of Knowledge', by Krishna Misra. It is an allegorical play in which practically all the characters are abstract notions and symbolical figures. Its main strength lies in the effectiveness of its moral and philosophical stanzas, but the action of its allegorical figures cannot be said to show any dramatic power. The dialogue is sometimes not without humour, and the author handles his favourite metres with skill; he also uses rimed verses in Prakrit. The whole play is a glorification of the cult of Vishnu as a form of orthodox Brahminism, much as the allegorical plays of the Spanish poet Calderon exalt the Catholic faith.

Krishna Misra had many imitators of this type of play in later centuries; but nearly all of them are without merit.

Other kinds of drama, which belong to modern times and have been preserved in great numbers, may be passed over here. But. two types, which have been very popular in India, though they have little literary value, may be mentioned. One of these, the Bhanas, all of which seem to come from southern India, deal with low life presented in the form of monologue. The Prahasanas, or farces, represent everyday life, in which rogues and various kinds of worthless characters indulge in altercations and fraudulent proceedings.

6.

Folklore

The narrative matter which we find treated in the court epics and the dramas based on ancient legends brings us to **the most valuable product of Indian literature, its folklore, which in India was earlier and to a wider extent raised to the rank of actual literature than among other nations of antiquity.** Such matter takes a prominent place, not only among the sacred books of the Buddhists and the Jains, but also among the works of Sanskrit literature. For us it is in many respects more valuable than all the other branches of Indian literary production. When we find how in the court epics and in the dramas the same old legendary material is, with few exceptions, treated over and over again, and similar plots recur with trifling changes, we are almost inclined to believe that the Indians show a complete lack of inventive power.

But the folklore literature introduces us to a world of infinite originality, in which the characters are no longer stereotyped, as in the epics and the drama, but are human beings with individual traits, not only heroic warriors, virtuous kings, and beautiful princesses, but people of the most. varied kind—peasants, merchants, artisans, and all sorts of doubtful characters, thieves, vagabonds, selfish Brahmins, hypocritical monks, courtesans, and procuresses. It is an imaginary world, full of marvellous and complicated fairy tales, of wit in the invention of serious and comic scenes, of wealth of fancy in the creation of ever new material in story and romance. This is in fact the most original department of Indian literature. It is also the one that has exercised a greater influence on foreign literatures than any other branch of Indian writing.

The history of how Indian fairy tales and fables migrated from one country to another, to nearly all the peoples of Europe and Asia, and even to African tribes, from their original home in India, borders on the marvellous. It is not a case of single stories finding their way by word of mouth through the agency of merchants and travellers from India to other countries, but of whole Indian books becoming through the medium of translations the common property of the world. After this had been demonstrated, it was at one time even believed that India was the source of all fairy tales, but the progressive study of folklore has irrefutably disproved such an assumption. It is, however, true that **many fairy tales current among the most various peoples can be traced to their original home in India.** Long before there were extensive collections of this character in Indian literature, all kinds of separate stories and fairy tales circulated among the people simply as a means of amusement, and also single fables invented by religious and secular teachers for the purpose of edification.

Fairy tales, stories, and anecdotes long in general circulation, and fables introduced in various parts of already existing literary works, became the sources or the models of the stories contained in folklore collections. Fairy tales have at all times, in India and elsewhere, supplied the place of what in our times is entertaining literature. This is what distinguishes the fairy tale from the myth, which endeavours to explain some physical problem or satisfy some religious doubt, while the fable is always intended to instruct and to point a moral. Fairy tales thus lived long among the people before they were introduced into literature in Prakrit books. The fable arose in literature itself, probably in Sanskrit from the beginning. The beast-fable, however, most likely originated in the beast fairy tale, a didactic maxim being combined with the story. For edification is always an essential element in the fable literature.

The earliest form of the literary narrative is a mixture of prose and verse. Certain stories are already found in Vedic literature, like that of Pururavas and Urvasi, but these belong to the sphere of myth and legend rather than to that of fairy tale in the strict sense. It was only in the later days of the post-Vedic period that works of literary narrative were composed entirely in verse. Works written entirely in prose are rare; in the historical romances verses are to a limited extent introduced.

The oldest actual fables in Indian literature are to be found in the *Mahabharata*. That fables existed in India as early as the third century B.C. is proved by the reliefs on the *stupa* of Bharhut, which dates from that time and on which the titles of many stories are engraved. Again, the Sanskrit grammarian Patanjali, in explaining the formation of certain compound words such as *kaka-taliya-vat*, 'like (the story of) the crow and the palm-tree', proves the same fact for the second century B.C.

The works comprising the narrative literature that

have come down to us may be grouped in two main classes, each of which includes two subdivisions. The first class is didactic in character. It consists (*a*) of collections of stories compiled for the purpose of religious edification: such were the Jatakas and other story-books of the Buddhists and the Jains written in Prakrit; (*b*) story-books written in Sanskrit for the express purpose of inculcating political doctrine and worldly wisdom: such was the *Panchatantra.* The second class embraces works written for the purpose of amusing. These were either (*a*) story-books, which were first composed in Prakrit, like the *Brahatkatha*, but later in Sanskrit, like the *Sukasaptati* or (*b*) novels and romances written in classical Sanskrit prose, like the *Dasakumara-carita* and the *Vasavadatta*.

All but the first of these four groups were the works of individual authors, who themselves invented them and in part derived their material from current stories or from other collections.

The general construction of these story-books was inter-calation, that is to say, the insertion of a group of stories within the framework of a single narrative. Within a subordinate story another could be similarly introduced and the process further repeated. This style of narration was borrowed from India by the Arabs, who employed it in composing works of their own. The most notable example is the *Arabian Nights,* into which several stories originally Indian have found their way.

The Panchatantra

The main book belonging to this department is the *Panchatantra,* which has had a longer and more eventful history than any other work of Indian literature. Two German scholars have been concerned with the elucidation of that history. Theodor Benfey was the first both to translate it from Sanskrit and to trace its migrations, by translation, into the literatures of almost innumerable countries. The second is Professor Johannes Hertel, who has, by means of critical editions of its most important recensions and by numerous researches, laid bare its fortunes in India itself. It is only natural that the original form of a text of this kind, consisting of a number of stories and maxims, should have undergone frequent alterations in the course of many centuries. But its original character was never quite effaced. It always remained a work intended to teach political science and worldly wisdom in the form of fables, stories, and maxims. In its earliest form it was a work for the instruction of princes, but later it became more a book for the education of youth generally. Purely moral stories were to a certain extent introduced only in later recensions. Although the original form of the *Panchatantra* has not been preserved, we are able to draw well-founded conclusions regarding it from its earliest surviving recensions. There are five such.

The *Tantrakhyayika,* or 'Treatise of Instructive Stories', is the form that best represents the original text. Two recensions of it have been preserved in Kashmir. Another is the text that was translated into Pehlevi in 570 A.D. Though both this text and the Pehlevi translation have been lost, the Syriac and Arabic versions from the Pehlevi and the European translations from the Arabic enable us to infer what the original Sanskrit text was like. Thirdly, there was an abstract of the *Panchatantra* contained in the lost Kashmirian work called the *Brihatkatha,* of which two metrical recensions have been preserved in Kshemendra's *Brihatkatha-manjari* and in

Somadeva's *Kathasaritsagara*; the latter of these throws more valuable light on the old text of the *Panchatantra*. There is further a greatly curtailed abstract generally called the South Indian *Panchatantra,* which is closely related to the *Tantrakhyayika* and has been shown to go back to an abstract made in northwest India after the seventh century A.D.

Finally, there is a Nepalese abstract of the stanzas contained in the *Panchatantra,* preserved in a single manuscript, nearly related to the Southern *Panchatantra* and going back to a north-western text. This, too, is of considerable critical importance. All these five are derived from a common original text of the *Panchatantra,* to which, however, the *Tantrakhyayika* appears to come nearest. Though the latter is a product of the artificial Sanskrit style of composition, its artificiality is moderate and falls far short of that of romances like those of Bana. The author was evidently a writer of ability and originality.

As to the age of the *Panchatantra,* we know that by the middle of the sixth century A.D. it was so famous that by order of the Sassanian king Khosru Anushirvan (531-79 A.D.) it was translated into Pehlevi and from Pehlevi into Syriac as early as 570. But research has hitherto been unable to prove when the original first came into being. Nothing more definite can be said than that it most probably arose between 300 and 500 A.D. There can be no doubt that in the form of the *Tantrakhyayika* it is one of the earliest products of the artificial literature of India. But as that recension contains undoubted interpolations, the date of the original *Panchatantra* must be still earlier. No chronological conclusions can be drawn from the religious and social conditions that it reflects. The general atmosphere is that of Brahminism, while no relation to Buddhism can be found in the book. The view once rather widely held that the *Panchatantra* was of Buddhist origin must therefore be rejected.

The most popular and most widespread in India of the old texts of the *Panchatantra* is designated the 'textus simplicior', which has also been the longest and best known in Europe. Before the discovery of the *Tantrakhyayika* it was regarded as the standard *Panchatantra*. It is, however, a completely new revision of the old work, in fact almost a new book; for many new stories and stanzas have been added in it, while many old stanzas are lacking. The style in this text is clear and simple, and the stories are told better and at greater length than in the *Tantrakhyayika*. The 'textus simplicior' ultimately goes back to the north-western text that was the basis both of the Pehlevi translation and of the abridgement forming the southern *Panchatantra*.

On the 'textus simplicior' is chiefly based the 'textus ornatior', which was produced in 1199 by a Jain monk named Purnabhadra. It is the best preserved of the later revisions of the *Panchatantra*. As compared with the older texts it contains many new stories and maxims.

The Hitopadesa

The most important of all the modern adaptations of the *Panchatantra* is the *Hitopadesa*, or 'Salutary Advice', which is widely diffused in Bengal and is best known in India and Europe. Though in fact a totally new work, its chief source is the *Panchatantra* in its north-western recension, which is also the source of the southern *Panchatantra*. About its date nothing more certain can be said than that it was composed between

1000 and 1300 A.D. Its place of origin was probably Bengal. The author is very independent in the way in which he has altered and rearranged the subject-matter. The *Hitopadesa* contains seventeen stories which are not found in any of the recensions of the *Panchatantra*. The character of a work on political science is more apparent in the *Hitopadesa* than in any other adaptation of the *Panchatantra*. It adds a large number of maxims of this type. The *Hitopadesa* is one of the works of Indian literature that has been known longest and best in Europe. Besides being extensively studied in the original, it has been translated into many Indian vernaculars, including Bengali, as well as repeatedly into European languages.

The *Panchatantra* itself has of course also been frequently translated into the Indian vernaculars. A Hindi version of it was known to the Arabic scholar Alberuni about 1030 A.D. It was also translated into Gujarati, Marathi, and the Dravidian languages of the south. The diffusion of translations outside India was much wider still. During many centuries the *Panchatantra* enriched in this way the literatures of three continents, and exercised an extraordinary influence on the narrative works of the whole Middle Ages. This was shown by Theodor Benfey in the introduction to his translation of the *Panchatantra*. He traced with extraordinary acuteness the migration of Indian stories in the most various languages of the East and West throughout the world. He thus became the founder of the comparative history of literature.

India presents a soil particularly favourable to the invention of fables, animal stories, and fairy tales. For here we find the belief in transmigration, which effaces the difference between the human and the animal worlds, and which thus renders it quite natural for animals to be the heroes of stories. Consequently no other country has produced so extensive a literature of stories as India. Thus not only single Indian tales but whole story-books are to be found in foreign literatures. We can very often even trace the actual routes by which fables and fairy tales have made their way from India throughout the world. By far the most important work of this type was the *Panchatantra.*

Translations into World Languages

The translation into Pehlevi, the literary language of medieval Persia, has indeed been lost, but the Syriac version made from that in 570 A.D, under the title of *Kalilag and Damnag,* though somewhat imperfectly preserved, is still extant. Another was the complete translation into Arabic (750 A.D.) entitled *Kalila and Dimna.* Both titles are distortions of the names of the two jackals, Karataka and Damanaka, that appear in the first book of the *Panchatantra.* This Arabic translation is the source to which the numerous versions, direct or indirect, found in European and Asiatic languages are to be traced. To be more precise, translations of the *Kalila and Dimna* have been made into forty languages, besides those from Sanskrit into fifteen Indian vernacular tongues. Probably no book except the Bible has been translated into so many languages, certainly no secular book. It has truly been said regarding this narrative literature that 'the story of the migration of Indian fairy tales from East to West is more wonderful and instructive than many of those fairy tales themselyes.

The best and most famous of the versions of *Panchatantra* in the Middle Ages was the German one of Anton von Pforr entitled 'Das Buch der Beispiele der alten Weisen', which first appeared in 1483, soon after the invention of printing, and was reprinted afterwards. For a long time it contributed most to a knowledge of the original in the whole of Europe. It not only influenced German literature in many ways, but was also itself translated into Danish, Icelandic, and Dutch. This German version was four times removed from the Arabic one which started the *Panchatantra* on its westward wanderings.

On the Latin translation of John of Capua (1263) was based a Spanish one (1493), from which was derived an Italian one in two parts (1552). The first of these parts was rendered into English by Sir Thomas North in 1570. This appeared exactly 1,000 years after the Syriac translation made from Pehlevi in 570 A.D. No fewer than six renderings intervened between it and the original Sanskrit text of the *Panchatantra*. The geographical separation between the starting-point and this goal was also one of the greatest. It appeared under the title of 'The Morall Philosophie of Doni'.

It is thus no wonder that the most popular European story-books contain traces of Indian fables and fairy tales, such as the *Gesta Romanorum,* the works of Boccaccio, Chaucer, and Lafontaine, and even, in the nineteenth century, Grimm's *Tales.* Some such stories have passed from literature into oral tradition in Europe, and have acquired a local colouring in their new home. An instance of this is the Welsh story of Llewellyn's dog Gelert, who, with his mouth besmeared witli blood, joyfully fawns on his master as he returns from the chase. Llewellyn rushes into the house to find his child's cradle overturned and traces of blood scattered about. But on examining the cradle he finds the child sleeping peacefully and a dead wolf lying by his side. This is the Welsh transformation of the *Panchatantra* story about the Brahmin who, having left a mongoose to guard his child in a cradle during his absence, returns and is greeted by the mongoose who rolls at his feet. But the Brahmin, seeing his mouth covered with blood, assumes he has bitten the child and kills him on the spot. Afterwards, finding the child uninjured and a dead serpent near him, he is overwhelmed with remorse.

When, however, stories are identical in East and West, while there is no evidence, from translations passing westward, of their Indian origin, we can only conjecture which side is the recipient. The same is the case when a fable is identical in Greece and India. There are several such, as that of the ass in the lion's skin. On this question there is great difference of opinion among scholars: some holding Greece, others India, to be the source of all; others again favour India, but admit that some fables must have come from Greece. The criteria seem here too subjective to justify definite conclusions. A weighty consideration is the fact that the Greek fable flourished as early as 500 B.C. in the time of Aesop, whom Herodotus (484-435 B.C.) knew as a writer of fables.

The oldest Indian fables go back only conjecturally to the fourth and fifth century B.C., and only a few with certainty to the third century B.C. But it by no means necessarily follows that those fables which the Indians have in common with the Greeks are certainly derived from the oldest period (sixth and fifth centuries B.C.) of Greek fables. The great majority both of the Aesopian and Indian fables may date from the time when there was an active intellectual interchange between Greece and India. Greek fables might then have easily come to India and Indian fables to Greece. This was the time, the third century A.D., when Babrius (*c.* 200 A.D.) wrote his collection of Aesopian fables. The truth probably is that the fable as a type did not arise exclusively either in India or in Greece, but that it came into being independently in each country, and that an interchange of individual fables between Greece and India took place when communication between the two countries arose.

Brihatkatha

According to the evidence of the romance writers, Dandin, Subandhu, and Bana, there existed in the sixth century A.D. a work of entertaining literature, which consisted of a collection of stories, the *Brihatkatha* by Gunadhya, written not in Sanskrit, but in Paisachi, a dialect probably of the north-west, and not otherwise used in literature. Though this work has not been preserved, two Sanskrit translations, made from it probably centuries later, have come down to us. These have been preserved in two recensions, the Kasmirian and the Nepalese. The former is known to us in two metrical forms, both of which date from the eleventh century. The earlier, Kshemendra's *Brihatkatha-manjari,* composed about 1037 A.D., is meant to be an abridgement of the *Brihatkatha*.

The later form of the Kasmirian recension, the *Katha-sarit-sagara,* or 'Ocean of Narrative Streams', was composed between 1063 and 1081 A.D. Though Somadeva writes in the Kavya style, he does not make an exaggerated use of poetic ornament or of metre, for he adapts the form to the matter. There can be no doubt that he is one of the most pleasing and skilful poets of India. It is likely that the defects of this work are due to the original *Brihatkatha*. The chief one is the faulty arrangement of the matter. Very often stories appear that do not suit the context, and the same story is found in two, occasionally even three, different forms. The main story is, moreover, much less interesting than those of which it is the framework. Somadeva evidently thought less of the latter than of the interwoven tales. He incorporated in it whole books, like the *Panchatantra,* as well as long, independent novels in which other shorter stories are inserted.

The *Kathasarit-sagara* throws much light on the contemporary social and religious conditions prevailing in India. It is also important in its relation to world-literature, for several of its stories reappear in the West.

The Nepalese recension of the *Brihatkatha* by Buddhasvamin, which is entitled *Brihatkatha-sloka-samgraha,* and is incomplete, seems more original than the Kasmirian recension. The arrangement and subject-matter differ so much from the latter, that in some places it seems quite another work.

Vetala-pancavimsatika

The *Vetala-pancavimsatika,* or 'Twenty-five (tales) of the Vetala', is a collection of stories which was contained in the Kasmirian recension of the *Brihatkatha,* for it appears both in Kshemendra's and Somadeva's poems. Its oldest form was lost, but Kshemendra and Somadeva preserve it in probably an older shape than that in which it has survived as a separate work. As such it exists in the two recensions of Sivadasa and Jambhaladatta. The former, who probably wrote in the twelfth century, seems to have handed down the more original form of the narrative, a mixture of prose and verse. The framework of this collection of stories is associated with a Vetala, or ghost infesting cemeteries, and magic plays an important part in these tales. This work, like the *Panchatantra,* has contributed many stories to world-literature.

A later, but also well-known and popular story-book is the *Simhasana-dvitrimsika,* 'Thirty-two Tales of the Throne', which is also entitled *Vikrama-carita,* or 'Career of Vikrama". It. is found in three recensions, one in prose, another in verse, and a third in a mixture of both. Of these, the South Indian prose recension probably comes nearest to the original form of the work. These thirty-two tales are very fantastic and fall far below the intellectual level of the *Vetala-pancavimsatika*. As King Bhoja of Dhara is mentioned in the main story forming the framework in every recension, the book cannot be earlier than 1000 A.D. It may, however, possibly have been composed in the reign of that ruler. It was translated into Persian in 1574 A.D., and there are many versions in Indian vernaculars, as well as in Siamese and Mongolian.

Suka-saptati

One of the most famous and popular Indian story-books *Suka-saptati*, 'Seventy Tales of a Parrot'. As is so often the case with such works, the original form of it must be regarded as irretrievably lost, though there are in existence many widely divergent recensions, translations into Indian vernaculars, and versions in foreign languages. The form in which it is composed is simple prose alternating with sententious verse, the latter being partly in Sanskrit, partly in Prakrit. Many of the maxims are to be found in other story-books, especially the

Panchatantra, and several of the tales, particularly the fables, are taken from that work. Nothing is known about the author or the time when it was composed. A fact of great importance in connexion with world-literature is that the *Suka-saptati* was translated into Persian early in the fourteenth century under the title of *Tutinameh.* The rough and uncouth quality of this rendering induced Nachshabi, a contemporary of Hafiz and Sadi, to mould its matter into an artistic poem. Based on the latter was another Persian version made in the seventeenth century, as well as a Turkish one dating from about a century after Nachshabi. Through the *Tutinameh* many Indian stories migrated to Western Asia and Europe. The best known of these was the tale of the fraudulent ordeal, rendered famous in Gottfried von Strassburg's 'Tristan und Isolde'. There were many later imitations of the *Suka-saptati* both in Sanskrit and the vernaculars.

Nearly related in matter to the *Suka-saptati* is the story of Sindbad, a famous tale of world-literature. It was probably based on an Indian original; for the Arabian writer Masudi (who died in 956 A.D.) said of the *Kitab el Sindbad,* 'Book of Sindbad', that it was derived from India. This work is essentially identical with tlie Persian *Sindibad-nameh,* the Syriac *Sindban,* an Arabic version contained in the 'Arabian Nights', the Hebrew *Sandabar,* the Greek *Syntipas,* and a number of other books in European languages. The introduction is Indian, quite similar to that of the *Panchatantra,* as well as the idea that the stories are told to save somebody's life. Most of the tales recur in some Indian story-book, as that of the death of the innocent mongoose in the *Panchatantra.* There can be no doubt that the 'Arabian Nights' are the result of Indian influence. All the main elements of its framework are derived from Indian ideas, and a large number of its stories are of Indian origin. The evidence, however, is not sufficient to prove that the Pehlevi original was a translation from Sanskrit. We cannot as yet reach a more definite conclusion than that a Persian poet composed the framework as well as a number of the tales, imitating Indian originals, of the 'Arabian Nights'.

Contemporary with the artificial epics, and composed not long before or after 600 A.D., were a few prose romances that are classed as Kavyas by the Sanskrit writers on poetics because, though not written in verse, they have all the characteristics of that style: descriptions filled with similes and figures of speech, immensely long compounds, puns, and other ornaments. Narrative here occupies a very subordinate place, being chiefly employed as the thread connecting a series of lengthy descriptions full of long strings of comparisons and often teeming with puns. Owing to the frequent use of immense compounds, their style makes them difficult reading. Their matter, however, is not derived from mythology or heroic legends, but mostly from the literature of fairy tales.

Dasakumara-charita

The earliest of these, the *Dasakumara-carita,* or 'Adventures of the Ten Princes', was written by Dandin and dates from the sixth century. It differs from Gunadhya's *Brihatkatha* by its elaborate Kavya style rather than by its matter. For it consists of stories and fairy tales enclosed in a framework. The narrative is so complicated that its thread can only be followed with difficulty. It is often dependent on arbitrary occurrences, such as a curse or dream, and not on inner necessity. The caprice of the fairy tale everywhere prevails. The erotic element is always prominent, the author being fond of dwelling on descriptions of female beauty or of love-scenes. Dandin shows himself to be a master of the most ornate Kavya style, which, however, he varies with simple unadorned narrative. The whole of the seventh chapter represents a trick of style, which excludes every labial sound from its diction. It is difficult to judge of the extent of Dandin's inventive power, because we do not know how much he borrowed from predecessors. His work is particularly interesting owing to the light it sheds on social life, especially the activity of the dishonest classes, such as vagabonds, thieves, gamblers, and courtesans. The daily life of a king is related with much detail in the story of Virabhadra in Chapter VIII. The work has been preserved in a somewhat incomplete form.

Subandhu, as the author of the romance *Vasavadatta* (the story of which has nothing to do with the plot of the play attributed to Bhasa), was famous as one of the best of poets. Of his life nothing is known, nor is any other work of his mentioned anywhere. The plan of the tale, which was probably not invented by him, contains features commonly occurring in fairy tales, such as love originating in a dream, speaking birds, magical horses, transformation into a pillar of stone, and so forth. His chief aim is not to invent stories of adventure, but to display his masterly skill in the Kavya style. His *Vasavadatta,* which recounts the popular story of a princess of Ujjayini bearing that name, was composed by Subandhu about 600 A.D. The author of two celebrated romances was Bana, the first Indian poet about whose date we have certain knowledge. He lived at the court of King Harshavardhana (606-48 A.D.) of Thanesar (in

Sanskrit Sthanesvara). He wrote his *Kadambari,* which relates the fortunes of a princess so named, early in the seventh century.

The story is borrowed from a fairly tale in the *Brihatkatha* of Gunadhya. The narrative consists of a series of stories one within another. The style is similar to that of the *Harsacarita,* but the story is less interesting. Though the patience of the reader is generally tried by the almost unendurable complexity of the diction, it is occasionally relieved by short sentences of natural, unstrained prose, as is the case in Subandhu's *Vasavadatta,* Though not to the same extent as the *Harsacarita,* the *Kadambari* throws much light on the manners and customs of the times, especially on the religious life of the adherents of the Sivaite sects.

The *Kadambari* remained uncompleted owing to the death of the author, but it was continued and finished by the poet's son in his father's style.

Kadambari

Bana's chief work is the *Harsacarita,* 'The Life and Doings of Harsha', a prose historical romance, in which a few verses are intermingled. Here Bana gives some account of the career of his patron Harsavardhana of Kanauj. This work contains many data that are of importance for literary and political chronology. Thus Bana mentions a number of his predecessors, including Subandhu, Satavahana (Hala), Bhasa, Kalidasa, Gunadhya, and some others. Though he scarcely equals Subandhu in the matter of puns and other literary devices, he is far superior to him in true poetical endowment. His work is a mixture of truth and fiction, the former of which is of some chronological value, being of Especial importance as illustrating the social and still more the religious conditions of the time. Himself a Brahmin, he mentions many sects, towards all of whom he is tolerant. But he does not refrain from criticizing the failings of religious men. Thus he remarks: 'A Brahmin who is not avaricious, a wandering ascetic who is not voracious, are hard to find.'

The first two chapters of the *Harsacarita* contain an autobiography supplying valuable information regarding the poet's life. But though the narrative is often of interest, it is much impeded by the great space given up to the description of persons, localities, and natural phenomena, teeming with similes and puns. Thus the panegyric of Harsha, when seen for the first time by Bana, occupies ten printed pages. The end of the work seems to have been lost.

Some idea of the style of these romances may be gained from the following quotation from the *Harsacarita* describing a disconsolate princess lying prostrate in a wood: 'Lost in the forest and in thought, bent upon death and the root of a tree, fallen upon calamity and her nurse's bosom, parted from her husband and happiness, burnt with the fierce sunshine and the woes of widowhood, her mouth closed with silence as well as by her hand, she was held fast by her companions as well as by grief. I saw her kindred and her graces all gone, her ears and her soul left bare, her ornaments and her aims abandoned, her bracelets and her hopes broken, her companions and needle-like grass-spears clinging round her feet, her eye and her beloved fixed within her bosom, her sighs and her hair long, her limbs and her merits exhausted, her aged attendants and her streaming tears falling at her feet,' and so forth.

There is no probability that the least influence was exercised on these romances by the Greek novel, or vice versa, as a literary type. But individual short stories or fairy tales may very well have been incorporated from the other on each side, especially as the result of oral interchange rather than of immediate literary borrowing.

There is a special kind of story-book called *champu,* in which verse in elaborate metres alternates with artificial prose, but without either predominating. The verse serves the same purpose as the prose: it is not here used, as, for instance, in the *Panchatantra,* to introduce sententious matter, or to summarize the story, or to emphasize important points. The best known of these works is the *Nala-champu* or *Damayanti-katha,* by Trivikrama Bhatta, whose date is known by an inscription of 915 A.D. Here the famous story of Nala and Damayanti is treated over again in this form.

7.

Technical Literature

ALL technical literature in India had its rise in theology. The study of the Vedic hymns early led to phonetic, grammatical, and metrical investigations as well as the beginnings of lexicography. Philosophy, developed in the Upanishads, was never completely dissociated from theology. Vedic ritual, requiring observation of the heavenly bodies, gave rise to the beginnings of astronomy. The construction of the sacrificial altar entailed measurements and led to geometry. Many of the spells of the *Atharvaveda* contain the germs of medical science. The regulation of sacrificial worship ended in religious science, which of course necessarily remained a branch of theology. With this was connected the science of *dharma*, concerned with religious and secular custom, which, gradually leaving the area of religion, developed into an extensive legal literature. **These were forms of technical knowledge which in their early stage were first studied in Vedic schools, but the development of departmental schools finally relegated the Vedic schools to the background.**

Only a few branches of secular science developed independently of theology: poetics (*alamkara*), the arts of practical life, especially that of government (*arthasastra*), and the art of love (*kamasastra*). The earliest form in which all science appeared in writing was the aphoristic prose style called *sutra*. The leading characteristic of the *sutra* and technical literature in general was a syntax in which substantives were almost exclusively used, and verbs practically disappeared. Another was fondness for abstract nouns and compounds. In connexion with the sutras was developed, an expository style, first probably in grammar and philosophy, of learned prose. Being based on the disputations, at assemblies of scholars, for the purpose of establishing a particular doctrine, **the technical literature of India has a scholastic and dialectical character almost throughout.** This style is often enlivened by illustrative analogies (*nyaya*). Thus an argument serving two purposes is stated to be used 'on the analogy of the lamp on the threshold', which shines in both directions, inwards and outwards. The oldest works in the department of technical science have seldom been preserved, because they were generally superseded by later commentaries or compendia.

Grammar

Grammar, called in Sanskrit *vyakarana*, or 'analysis', is by the Indians regarded as the first and most important of the sciences because it is the foundation of all of them. **The greatest achievement of Indian science, it has rendered eminent services to Western philology. The Sanskrit grammarians of India were the first to analyse word-forms, to recognize the difference between root and suffix, to determine the functions of suffixes, and on the whole, to elaborate a grammatical system so accurate and**

complete as to be unparalleled in any other country. Grammatical study began with the linguistic investigation of the Vedic hymns. Sakalya's Pada text of the *Rigveda,* in which not only the words of the sentence but the parts of compounds and even of certain inflected word-forms are separated, presupposes grammatical analysis. The following line of the *Rigveda* as it appears in the Samhita text, *gomataro yac chubhayante anjibhis*, becomes *go-matarah, yat, subhayante, anji-bhih*, in the Pada text.

The phonetic works called Pratisakhyas and Sikshas may be regarded as grammatical treatises. Technical grammatical terms occur in the Brahmanas, the Aranyakas, and the Upanishads, and Yaska's *Nirukta* shows that a considerable grammatical development had taken place by his time; but no actual grammar has come down to us from the Vedic period. The oldest grammatical work in Sanskrit is the celebrated grammar (*sabdanusasana*, or 'doctrine of words') of Panini in eight sections. It deals with Vedic grammar in the form of exceptions to Classical Sanskrit. The basis of his grammar is the usage of the Brahmanas, Upanishads, and Sutras rather than that of Classical Sanskrit. The date of Panini is usually assumed to be about 350 B.C., but the evidence for this is very doubtful: it is perhaps safer to say that he lived after, probably soon after, 500 B.C. His birthplace was Salatura in the north-west, near the present Attock.

Panini mentions ten predecessors by name, but his work was of such pre-eminent merit that it superseded all of them. His grammar has always been highly esteemed by the Indians, and has filled all Western scholars who have studied it with admiration. **His rules are expressed with algebraic brevity.** For instance, his last rule is:

'ă ă'. This means that 'short ă *is* in this grammar treated as if it were the short form of long *ā,* though it is really pronounced like a close short ă' (as the *u* in English *bŭt*). A characteristic feature of Panini's system is that he derives all words from verbal roots. It was formerly held by various Western scholars that Panini's system treated many roots and forms as existent that did not actually occur in the language, and that he had an inadequate knowledge of the Veda; but this view has been refuted.

The language that Panini's successors, Katyayana and Patanjali, had in view was essentially Classical Sanskrit. Patanjali is the author of the *Mahabhasya,* 'The Great Commentary', which does not discuss Panini's rules, but Katyayana's *varttikas,* which are short criticisms on about one-third of Panini's sutras. In these *varttikas* Katyayana criticizes the rules of Panini, not by any means in a hostile spirit, as was once thought, but with a view to correct or supplement them quite impartially, and he seldom rejects them. Patanjali is mainly concerned with explaining and criticizing the *varttikas;* but he also continues Katyayana's work in examining Panini's sutras in his *Mahabhasya.* The latter is the oldest extant work in the expository or Bhashya style, which here takes the form of an actual conversation, like a direct and often very lively dialogue. The language is simple and clear, and the sentences are short. The date of Patanjali has been much debated, but the view is now generally accepted that he lived in the second century B.C. It is certain that a considerable interval must have elapsed between Katyayana and Patanjali, and a still greater one between Panini and Katyayana. It is therefore a good working theory to assign Panini to 450 B.C., Katyayana to 350 B.C., and Patanjali to 150 B.C.

These three names bring the development of the science of Sanskrit grammar to a conclusion. We have no knowledge of their predecessors, while the later Indian grammarians have added nothing new. For they did not write about Sanskrit grammar directly, but only about the grammatical rules of Panini.

The best commentary on the complete sutras of Panini is the *Kasika Vritti,* 'The Commentary of Benares', by Jayaditya and Vamana, the former of whom died not later than 662 A.D. This work is distinguished by both brevity and clearness.

In 1635 A.D. Bhattoji Dikshita wrote the *Siddhdnta-kaumudi,* or 'Moonlight of Settled Conclusions', in which the sutras of Panini are arranged according to subjects, such as phonetics and declension, and commented on concisely and clearly. It is easy to understand and well adapted as an introduction to the Indian system of grammar.

An abridgement of this work is the *Laghu-kaumudi* of Varadaraja.

A philosophic grammarian was Bhartrihari, who died in 651 A.D. He wrote the *Vakyapadiya,* which deals with grammar from the point of view of the science of language. A good many treatises and commentaries deal with grammatical works supplementary to Panini. Such is Nagoji-bhatta's *Paribhasendu-sekhara,* which is concerned with the *paribhasas* or interpretative key-rules to Panini's grammar. The versified *Ganaratna-mahodadhi,* 'The Ocean of Gems of Word-groups', treats the *ganas* or lists of words to which grammatical sutras apply. It was written about 1140 A.D. by Vardhamana. One of the supplements to Panini is the *Unadi-sutras,* which give rules for the derivation of certain nouns from verbal roots by particular suffixes enumerated in a list beginning with *un,* that is, *u.* The best commentary on this is by Ujjvaladatta, who flourished about 1350 A.D. The *Phit-sutras* give rules for the accents of the Vedic language as well as of Sanskrit. These rules are by Santanava, who lived after Panini and was probably unknown to Patanjali.

The earliest of grammatical works which, though unable to emancipate themselves from Panini, aimed at forming new systems, is the *Ka-tantra* of Sarvavarman. It is an elementary work, well suited for beginners, dating probably from about 300 A.D. A commentary written on it is mentioned by Alberuni. The *Chandra-vyakarana,* the grammar of Chandragomin, is the Sanskrit grammar best known in the Buddhist countries of Kashmir, Nepal, Tibet, and Ceylon. The author utilized both the sutras of Panini and the commentary of Patanjali. His grammar was composed about 600 A.D.

Sakatayana's grammar, the *Sakatayana-vyakarana,* which makes use of Panini and the *Mahabhasya* as well as the grammar of Chandragomin, and employs the technical terms partly of Panini and partly of Chandragomin, was composed by the grammarian Sakatayana, a namesake of one of Panini's predecessors, in the ninth century A.D.

The grammar of Hemachandra, which is really an improved edition of Sakatayana, is more practical in arrangement and terminology than the works of Panini, Chandragomin, and Sakatayana. Being meant for Jains it does not of course deal with the Vedic language and the rules of accent.

There are various other grammars that have only a local popularity. The most widely known one in Bengal is the *Mugdhabodha* of Vopadeva, which differs from Panini both in arrangement and in technical terminology. The author lived in the second half of the thirteenth century.

The system of Panini was transferred to Prakrit, which was regarded simply as a literary language derived from Sanskrit. The oldest Prakrit grammar extant is the *Prakrita-prakasa* of Vararuchi. That it was a comparatively old work appears from the fact that Bhamaha (*c.* 650 A.D.), the earliest writer of a treatise on poetics (*alamkara*), composed a commentary on it. Vararuchi treats of only four Prakrit dialects, Maharashtri, Paisachi, Magadhi, and Sauraseni. He and all later grammarians start from the assumption that Maharashtri is the real and best Prakrit because it is nearest to Sanskrit. One of the older works is the *Prakrita-laksana* of Chanda, a treatise which is of uncertain date, and the text of which has been very badly preserved.

Hemachandra also wrote a Prakrit grammar which, though largely based on the work of predecessors, is the most important because of its comprehensiveness and the abundance of its linguistic material. He deals with three other dialects in addition to the four of Vararuchi, besides including the Jain form of Maharashtri. It is interesting to note that for Paisachi he quotes passages from the no longer existing *Brihatkatha* of Gunadhya.

The value of the Prakrit grammars has been very seriously questioned, but not always with justice. At least the earlier ones are indispensable to our knowledge of the Prakrit dialects, for the purpose of understanding both Prakrit poetry and the Prakrit portions of the dramas.

The Pali grammarians of Ceylon and Burma, similarly deriving their material exclusively from the literature, have slavishly followed the model of Sanskrit grammar. The oldest Pali grammar is that of Katyayana, the *Kaccayana-ppakarana.* He differs from others in treating Pali as an independent language, not as derived from Sanskrit; yet he uses the terminology of Sanskrit grammar, and frames his sutras on that model. He has utilized Panini and his successors (including the *Kasika-vrtti*) as well as the *Ka-tantra.* His work seems to date from between 500 and 1000 A.D. After 1000 A.D., when it began to be studied in Burma, Pali became the vehicle, in that country, of grammatical works on the language.

Lexicography

The origin of Sanskrit lexicography is to be traced to the Vedic Nighantus; but the real dictionaries, called by the name of *kosa* ('treasury' of words), are separated from these by a long interval. The transition is formed by the *Dhatu-pathas,* or 'Lists of Roots', and the *Gana-pathas,* or 'Lists of Word-groups'. The Nighantus contain verbs as well as nouns, but the Kosas only nouns and indeclinables. The Nighantus, again, relate to individual Vedic texts only, while the Kosas have no specific reference. The dictionaries are collections of rare and important words and meanings for the use of poets. Themselves written in verse (chiefly in the *sloka* metre), they are, like the treatises on poetics (*alamkara*), indispensable aids to poetical composition. They are of a general character, for they contain the technical terms of other literary departments, such as astronomy.

There are two kinds of dictionaries: the synonymous and the homonymous. The synonymous class embraces groups of words systematically arranged according to subjects that have the same meaning; for instance, all words expressive of 'earth'. The homonymous class comprises words with more than one meaning, which, as well as the gender, is often indicated by the locative case; for instance, *dine* = 'in (the sense of) day'; *trisu*, 'in three (genders)' = 'adjective'. The fact that the arrangement is not generally alphabetical is due to the dictionaries being intended to be learnt by heart and not to be looked up. The older dictionaries, which are known to us only in a fragmentary way, are quite unsystematic and prolix in their definitions, the explanation often occupying a whole couplet (*sloka*). Many are known from quotations in commentaries only. The *nama-linganusasana* of Amarasimha, generally called the 'Dictionary of Amara', or *Amara-kosa*, superseded nearly all the predecessors of Amara. The author was a Buddhist, though he does not specially favour the Buddhist vocabulary. Nothing certain is known of his date, but the probability is that he lived between 550 and 750 A.D. His work is a dictionary of synonyms in three sections. Of the fifty commentaries on this lexicon, few are known, the best being that of Bhatta Kshirasvamin, who probably lived *c.* 1050 A.D.[1]

A supplement to the *Amara-kosa* is the *Trikanda-sesa* of Purushottama-deva. It is one of the most important and interesting extant Indian lexicon, containing as it does many words peculiar to Buddhistic Sanskrit, as well as inscriptional and even Prakrit words. Its author also

1. The first English Thesaurus was made by Roget, who in his preface declares that he got the idea from Amar Singh's work. (Ed.)

compiled a concise lexicon, both synonymous and homonymous, entitled *Haravali,* or 'String of Pearls', which contains more rare words than the former work. Nothing is known of his date, but it cannot well have been far removed from 700 A.D.

Old and important is the *Anekartha-samuccaya,* a homonymous lexicon by Sasvata. An indication of its antiquity is its arrangement; for it begins with words the explanation of which requires a whole *sloka;* then follow those that need a half, and lastly those that take up one-fourth couplet; then come supplements and a section on indeclinables.

The earliest old lexicon that is approximately datable is the *Abhidhana-ratna-mala* of Halayudha, who wrote about 950 A.D. It is short, consisting of only 900 couplets. One of the most extensive lexicons is the *Vaijayanti* of Yadava-prakasa, another South Indian, who lived about a century later. The words are arranged according to the number of their syllables, then by the gender, and in every subdivision according to the initial. It is of great importance because it contains many words not to be found in other dictionaries.

Between, 1133 and 1140 A.D. a Digambara Jain named Dhananjaya wrote a lexicon entitled *Nama-mala* or 'Garland of Nouns'. The poet Mahesvara compiled the homonymous *Visvaprakasa* in the year 1111 A.D. as he himself states. Another poet named Mankha composed his *Anekartha-kosa,* accompanied by a commentary, about 1150 A.D.

Of the greatest importance are Hemachandra's dictionaries, which, according to his own statement, he compiled as supplements to his grammar. His lexicon of synonyms is the *Abhidhana-cintamani,* which consists of an introduction dealing with the different classes of words, and of six sections enumerating the Jain gods, the Brahmin gods, men, animals, denizens of the lower regions, while the last is concerned with abstracts, adjectives, and particles. As a supplement to this lexicon he compiled the *Nighantu-sesa,* which is a botanical glossary in 396 slokas. He also wrote the *Anekartha-samgraha,* a dictionary of homonyms in seven sections, of which the first six deal with substantives and adjectives according to the number of their syllables, while the seventh treats of indeclinables.

Of later lexicographical works, only two homonymous dictionaries need be mentioned. About 1200 A.D. Kesava-svamin compiled the *Nanartha-samkalpa,* in which the words are well arranged according to the number of syllables, the alphabet, and the gender. The much-quoted *Nanartha-sabda-kosa of* Medinikara probably dates from the fourteenth century. It is generally called *Medini-kosa* or simply *Medini*. It seems to have been based chiefly on the *Visvaprakasa*.

There are also several special glossaries. Some are associated with particular Buddhist Sanskrit works, resembling the Vedic Nighantus as being intended for individual texts and not having a metrical form. The oldest extant Prakrit dictionary is the *Paiya-lacchi-nama-mala* of Dhanapala written in 379 *arya* stanzas and dated 972 A.D. The words are here not arranged on any particular system, except that they begin with the names of gods and of sacred objects. This work was used by Hemachandra in his *Desi-nama-mala,* or 'Glossary of Provincial Words', as distinct from *tat-samas* or pure Sanskrit words and from *tad-bhavas,* or words derived from Sanskrit. It is very important for the study of Prakrit, because the dictionaries on which Hemachandra's work is founded have not been preserved.

The only early Pali dictionary extant is the *Abhidhana-ppadipika,* or 'Lamp of Words', of Moggallana. Dating from about 1300 A.D., and composed in verse, it follows completely the model of the *Amara-kosa.*

Philosophy

Philosophy, in Sanskrit termed *Anviksiki,* or 'science of research', has during a period of more than 2,000 years never succeeded in becoming independent of religion in India. The systems called *darsanas* ('views') are not merely the doctrines of particular philosophical schools, but of particular religious sects. The Indians generally consider these systems to be six in number, consisting of three more closely associated pairs. These are regarded as orthodox because they hold the Veda to be the principal means of knowledge. They are the *Purva-* and *Uttara-mimamsa;* the *Sankhya* and *Yoga*; the *Nyaya* and *Vaisesika*. The Jain Haribhadra substituted for the first and fourth Buddhism and Jainism. These eight as well as other systems, altogether sixteen, are critically described in the *Sarva-darsana-samgraha*, 'Compendium of all Philosophical Systems', by the great Vedanta scholar Madhava (fourteenth century), brother of the famous Vedic commentator Sayana.

Philosophy as a whole is not regarded as a *sastra* or branch of knowledge, like grammar and others, but each individual system or *darsana* is one in itself. The literature of each of these *sastras* consists of a *sutra* work as its foundation, and a succession of commentaries. But the date of none of these fundamental texts can be traced with certainty, nor is anything known about their authors, who are nothing but names, some of which seem to be actually mythical. The basic *sutras,* which form the starting-point of a system, in reality represent the end of a long and extensive literary development that has been lost. They are all the productions of schools, not of individuals. Even if we could determine the date of the *sutras,* this would prove nothing regarding the time when the philosophical systems and schools came into being. Thus, though the *Sankhya-sutra* is the latest of all philosophical *sutras,* the Sankhya philosophy as reduced to a system is regarded as the oldest.

The Purva- and the Uttara-mimamsa

Most closely connected with the Vedic religion are the two systems called the *Purva-mimamsa* and the *Uttara-mimamsa,* the latter better known under the name of *Vedanta.* They are the real philosophy of orthodox Brahmanism, the ultimate appeal of which is the Veda. The former means 'the discussion of the first (practical) part', the latter, 'the discussion of the second (theoretical) part' of the Veda, which is concerned with the doctrine of the world-soul. The *Purva-mimamsa* was originally concerned with the rules (*nyaya*) for the correct interpretation of the texts relating to ritual acts. There must have been such rules centuries before Christ; but it by no means follows that the fundamental text, the *Purva-mimamsa-sutra* of Jaimini, goes back to such an early time. Here no other way of salvation is laid down but that of works, that is, of sacrifices and ceremonies, and no higher authority for religious duties (*dharma*) than the Veda. These *sutras* contain little of what we would consider philosophy. Their importance consists in their representing the method of discussion which has been adopted in the whole of the philosophical and scientific literature of India.

The oldest extant commentary is that of Sabara-svamin, who quotes a predecessor named Upavarsha, probably belonging to the fifth century A.D. He combats the two philosophical systems of the Buddhists. Two schools of interpretation of Sabara's commentary grew up. The more famous scholar representing one of them was Kumarila, who wrote a very extensive commentary in three parts on Sabara-svamin's work. It is full of hair-splitting learning and acuteness. His polemics are directed chiefly against the Buddhists, who denied the authority of the Veda. Written about 700 A.D., it is of great importance owing to the many references it contains to contemporary literature and social life. Kumarila was a south Indian, and had a knowledge of the Dravidian languages. A later manual was the *Nyaya-mala-vistara* of the famous Vedanta scholar Madhava. There was an original opposition between the *Purva-* and the *Uttara-mimamsa,* because the former regarded works, the latter knowledge, as the only means of salvation; but finally their antagonism became merged in their common Brahmanic orthodoxy.

The basic text of the *Uttara-mimamsa* is the *Vedanta-sutra* ascribed to Badarayana. It must have been constituted contemporaneously with that attributed to Jaimini, because these two authors refer to each other's works. The *Vedanta-sutra* contains only catchwords, unintelligible without a commentary; and as there is no uninterrupted tradition between Badarayana and Sankara, whose commentary is the oldest extant, it is not always certain what Badarayana's doctrine was. It appears, however, to be undoubted that one of the main doctrines of the later Vedanta, that of *maya,* which holds the phenomenal world to be an illusion, has not yet been developed in the *Vedanta-sutra.* It is first met with in the *Karikas* of Gaudapada, which, excepting the *sutras,* are among the earliest products of Vedanta literature.

Sankara, the chief of the Vedanta philosophers, was the principal exponent of the *a-dvaita* ('non-dualistic') doctrine, or strict monism. He distinguished a lower kind of knowledge suited to the comprehension of the many, and a higher kind which met the requirements of strict philosophic thought. His chief works were commentaries on the Upanishads, the *Bhagavadgita,* and the *Vedanta-sutra.* Many other works, of which he was not the author, are attributed to him. We know nothing about his life, but in all probability he flourished from about 800 A.D. onwards.

Every word of the Upanishads is irrefutable truth to both Badarayana and to Sankara, but they differ in their interpretation. The style of Sankara is no longer that of a living disputation, but rather that of a scientific treatise. His sentences are long and involved. But his exposition is clear and transparent compared with that of the later philosophic commentaries. His *Gitabhasya,* or 'Commentary on the *Bhagavadgita*', is rather an independent religio-philosophic treatise than a commentary in the strict sense. From the *Gita* he tries to adduce proofs for his own doctrine, especially its exoteric part relating to the performance of social duties.

Of his other works may be mentioned the *Atmabodha,* a compendium of the Vedanta doctrine in sixty-seven stanzas, with an appended commentary. The subsequent literature of Sankara's monistic doctrine is very extensive. One of the most devoted of his followers was Madhava, who wrote the *Pancadasi,* the most popular exposition of the Vedanta in the India of to-day.

The best known and favourite short handbook of the Vedanta, serving as an excellent introduction to the system, is the *Vedanta-sara,* 'The Quintessence of the Vedanta', by Sadananda, who must have lived before or soon after 1500 A.D., as commentaries on his work were already written in the sixteenth century. In this treatise Sankhya ideas are found intermingled with the Vedanta framework of the system.

As the followers of Sankara also formed a religious sect, so the other Vedanta schools represent as many religious sects. The next in importance to the adherents of Sankara were those of Ramanuja, who, in propounding the doctrine of 'qualified monism', sought to combine with belief in one deity the doctrine of the love of God (*bhakti*). Ramanuja's activity ranges between 1175 and 1250 A.D. He was a south Indian, a native of Conjeeveram. The names of his father, mother, and teachers are known. Originally a monist, he became the founder of the theistic Vaishnava sect of south India. His chief work is the *Sribhasya,* or 'Glorious Commentary'.

Though a convinced believer in the truth of the Upanishads and of the *Vedanta-sutras,* he combated the views of Sankara on the relation of action and knowledge, on true knowledge, on the mutual connexion between Brahman and the world, on salvation, and so on. His chief aim, the reconciliation of the doctrines of the Upanishads, the *Bhagavadgita,* the *Mahabharata,* and the Puranas, with his own religion and philosophy, was theological rather than philosophical. To Ramanuja the legendary Vyasa was the seer and arranger not only of the Veda and the *Mahabharata,* but of the *Vedanta-sutras* as well. He assumes three principles: the individual soul, the inanimate world, and God as the Supreme Soul. His theories of the external world are based on the Sankhya philosophy and the Puranas. His doctrine of devotion (*bhakti*) to a personal deity he sought to combine with his conception of nature. In addition to his chief work, Ramanuja also wrote the *Gita-bhasya,* a commentary on the *Bhagavadgita.*

A well-known founder of a religious sect was Madhva (1197-1276), who wandered about the country preaching his doctrine. He wrote commentaries on the seven old Upanishads, the *Vedanta-sutra,* the *Bhagavadgita,* and the *Bhagavata Purana,* as well as a number of independent works. By very forced interpretations of the texts he endeavoured to reconcile his dualistic conception of the world by combining the Vedanta with the Sankhya system and the Bhagavata religion. He summarized the doctrines of his dualistic Vedanta in his *Tattva-sankhyana.* He wrote as a strenuous opponent of Sankara.

The founder of another sect was Vallabha (1478-1530), who was devoted to the cult of Krishna. He wrote a commentary on the *Vedanta-sutra* entitled *Anubhasya.*

The Vedanta philosophy allied itself not only with Vishnuite, but with Sivaite sects. Here, too, we find that the original monistic doctrine branches off in dualistic and Bhakti directions.

The Sankhya System

The earliest philosophical ideas are to be found in the Veda, and later the doctrines regarding Brahman and

Atman in the Upanishads, but the oldest philosophy that was elaborated as a system was the Sankhya, or 'enumerative philosophy', so called because classification of principles is characteristic of the system. It is the philosophy of realism, which arose in opposition to the idealism of the Upanishads.

The doctrine of Kapila, the legendary founder of the system, was independent of the authority of the Veda. For it was not based, like the Vedanta, on the interpretation of Vedic writings. It was only later that it attached itself to Brahmanism. For the founder rejects the conception of Brahman and the world-soul. He distinguishes matter, which is real, and an infinite plurality of individual souls, which are not regarded as emanations of a single world-soul. The ultimate cause of the world is primeval matter (*prakrti*), which in spite of its oneness consists of three constituent elements called *gunas.* Suffering arises from the non-distinction of soul and matter; but discriminative knowledge causes deliverance from suffering. The Sankhya is thus not only a system explaining the world, but also a method of salvation. But of all these doctrines there is nothing in Vedic literature; they thus form a direct contrast with those of the Veda. The teaching of the Sankhya, however, already exercised some influence, on the second chronological stratum of the Upanishads: the *Katha,* the *Svetasvatara,* the *Prasna,* and the *Maitri.*

There is a mixture of Sankhya with Vedanta doctrines in the philosophical sections of the *Mahabharata,* the Puranas, and the *Dharma-sastra* of Manu. The Sankhya indeed pervades the Puranas to such an extent that what is generally called 'Epic philosophy' might more correctly be styled 'Puranic philosophy'. It cannot be doubted that Buddha grew up in the atmosphere of Sankhya thought, for it is the essential basis of his world-view. There seems, in fact, good reason to believe that the Sankhya doctrine came into being as a system between 800 and 550 B.C. That it spread in early times beyond the confines of India is indicated by the Sankhya parable of the co-operation of the blind and the lame man being known in China in the second century B.C.

The oldest and completely preserved work of the Sankhya philosophy is the *Sankhya-karika* of Isvara-krishna. This work, with a commentary, was translated into Chinese between 557 and 569 A.D. It seems not unlikely that both text and commentary were anterior to the Buddhist teacher Vasubandhu, and came into existence about 300 A.D. It is written in the *arya* metre, and presents a clear exposition of the Sankhya doctrine. A very competent judge, the late French Sanskritist Auguste Barth, regarded it as the pearl of the whole scholastic literature of India. The account given of the Sankhya doctrine by the Arabic scholar Alberuni in 1030 A.D. is based on this work.

The most valuable commentary on the *Sankhya-karika,* and at the same time the best methodical account of the Sankhya doctrine in general, is the *Sankhya-tattva-kaumudi* of Vachaspati Misra.

The *Sankhya-sutra*, or *Sankhya-pravacana,* probably dates, in the form in which we possess it, from the fifteenth century, but is in all likelihood based on an older *Sahkhya-sutra* that was known many centuries earlier. Its oldest commentary, the *Sankhya-sutra-vritti,* was written about 1500 A.D. by Aniruddha.

About 1550 A.D, was composed the *Sankhya-pravacana-bhasya* by Vijnana-bhikshu, who as a strict Vedanta theist gives a forced interpretation of the *Sankhya-*

sutra in conformity with his own views. He divides the doctrine of salvation into four parts, probably suggested by the four noble truths of Buddhism. This division, however, seems to be ultimately derived from Indian medical science, which separates its subject-matter into the four sections of disease, health, cause of disease, and cure, as Vijnana-bhikshu himself tells us.

The Yoga System

While the Sankhya arose independently of religious belief, the Yoga was the immediate result of religious needs. Its origin may be traced to pre-Vedic ideas. The primary meaning is the 'yoking' of the mind with a view to concentrate thought on a single point; for these exercises aim at the regulation of breathing, sitting, and restraining the senses for the purpose of exclusive concentration on a single supernatural object, in order to obtain as a result supernatural knowledge and supernatural powers. Such practices are prehistoric, going back to a time when there was no essential difference between a saint and a magician.

That they were pre-Buddhistic in India appears from the great part these exercises play in ancient Buddhism. As restraint of the senses forms part of them, they evidently include morality. In this aspect, Yoga could be combined with any philosophical system. In one form or another, Yoga is to be found among all Indian ascetics, including Buddhists and Jains. As a system it became closely associated with the Sankhya, from which it differs only in its ascetic practice and in its adoption of theism. But its connexion with belief in a god is a somewhat loose one. The god (*isvara*) of the Yoga system does not create, reward, or punish. He is only a separate soul which is eternally combined with the most subtile constituent of matter, thus possessing the attributes of power, goodness, and wisdom. Devotion to God is only one element in Yoga morality (*kriyayoga*). Its philosophical basis is otherwise entirely the Sankhya system. Hence *Sankhya-pravacana* is the common title of the *Sankhya-sutra* and the *Yoga-sutra.*

The *Yoga-sutra,* the foundation of the Yoga philosophy, is ascribed to Patanjali, who, however, is probably not identical with the grammarian, the author of the *Mahabhasya.* It consists of four sections, which deal with the nature of concentration, the means of concentration, the miraculous powers acquired by concentration, and salvation, which consists in the isolation (*kaivalya*) of the soul. The philosophy of the system is contained in the commentaries. The oldest of these is the *Yoga-bhasya,* ascribed to the legendary Vyasa, and probably dating from about 500 A.D. This work was further commented on by Vachaspati Misra, Vijnana-bhikshu, and King Bhoja (eleventh century). To a later period belong the treatises on *hatha-yoga* or 'strict Yoga', which are practical manuals giving rules on the external aspects of Yoga, such as postures, breathing, diet, and so on, as opposed to the *raja-yoga,* 'royal Yoga' of Patanjali, which is chiefly concerned with meditation.

The Nyaya and Vaiseshika Systems

More closely complementary than the Sankhya and Yoga were the two systems called Nyaya and Vaiseshika, which finally coalesced to a single principle. Being essentially independent of religious belief, **they may be described as strictly scientific systems of logic and the theory of knowledge.**

Nyaya properly means 'method', applicable to any kind of argumentation. Disputations and learned contests play such a part in ancient India that a system of dialectics called *nyaya-sastra,* a body of rules for correct thinking, arguing, and inferring was naturally developed. The founder of the Nyaya system and author of the *Nyaya-sutra* is by tradition unanimously reputed to have been Akshapada Gotama. It cannot, however, be doubted that the *Sutra* attributed to him is the work of a school, not of an individual man. Its original form must also have undergone modifications and interpolations. It consists of five books, of which the first two deal with logic and the theory of knowledge and dialectics; the third with psychology; the fourth with rebirth and salvation; while the fifth is a supplement. It may date from about 300 A.D. in its latest shape, but its original form must be much older. There is a very old commentary, the *Nydya-sutra-bhasya,* which bears a certain likeness to Patanjali's *Mahabhasya,* by Pakshila-svamin Vat-syayana, who lived not improbably about 350 A.D.

The whole orthodox Nyaya-sastra consists of five works: the *Sutra,* its commentary, and three super-commentaries. The *Nyayasutra-bhasya* was commented on by Uddyotakara, who is quoted by the poet Subandhu, and who himself quotes the Buddhist logician Dharmakirti. The latter lived about 635 A.D. and on his part refers to Uddyotakara. Hence it is highly probable that these three writers were contemporaries about 635 to 650 A.D. Udayana, a highly esteemed writer on Nyaya and Vaiseshika, lived in the tenth century, one of his works being dated 984 A.D. He was the author of the *Kusumanjali,* or 'Handful of Blossoms' (on the tree of

Nyaya). This work aims at proving the existence of God from the Nyaya point of view. The author especially attacks the atheistical doctrine of the Mimamsakas as well as the law of causality in the Vedanta, in the Sankhya, and in Buddhism. He also wrote a special polemical work against the Buddhists.

The five works mentioned above constitute the 'old school' of logic. The great Buddhist logician Dignaga inaugurated the medieval school. This is chiefly represented by Buddhist and Jain scholars. Many of their works are only preserved in Tibetan translations. A pupil of Dharmapala, who before 635 A.D. had been head of the school at Nalanda, was Dharmakirti. He wrote the *Nyaya-bindu,* to which Dharmottara, who lived about 800 A.D. in Kashmir, composed a commentary.

The famous Jain scholar Hemachandra wrote a work on logic entitled *Pramana-mimamsa* in the *sutra* style. The 'new school' of logic at Navadvipa in Bengal begins with the *Tatva-cintamani,* a systematic treatise on the Nyaya, by Gangesa, written about 1200 A.D. After this the Nyaya system degenerated into a very barren scholasticism.

An extremely useful glossary of Nyaya technical terms is the *Nyaya-kosa,* which was compiled at the instigation of Professors Buhler and Kielhorn in 1874.

The Vaiseshika system which, independently of religious belief, endeavoured to explain the origin of the world from atoms, seems to have been akin to the *lokayata* materialistic philosophy. The Nyaya and Vaiseshika were the philosophy of non-theological scholars and 'heretics'. It is significant that the Buddhists and Jains had a considerable share in their development. There is a close affinity between the Vaiseshika and the Jain philosophy. The former may have arisen before the Jain and the Buddhist canon, about the second century; but the *Vaisesika-sutra,* which is the basis of the system, and the authorship of which is attributed to Kasyapa Kanada, is certainly not so old in its extant shape.

In this form it is a Brahmanic work with a religio-ethical tendency. But there can be little doubt that **it was originally a purely secular scientific work, which was later turned into an orthodox Brahmanical text** in a quite superficial manner. No old commentary of the *Vaisesika-sutra* has been preserved. The *bhasya* of Prasastapada entitled *Padartha-dharma-samgraha* probably dates from about 700 A.D., and is really an independent manual in which the subject-matter is systematically arranged. It is at the present day acknowledged as their text-book by adherents of both Nyaya and Vaiseshika. The commentary with which in 991 A.D. Sridhara supplied this work was the first Vaiseshika text to set forth theism formally. The first commentary, in the strict sense, on the *Vaisesika-sutra* was the *Upaskara* of Sankara Misra. It seems to have little value, for, as it was written as late as about 1600 A.D., the tradition of the original interpretation had long died out.

There is a great mass of commentaries and other works on the Nyaya and Vaiseshika which, in the later period, are indistinguishable. This literature tends rather to obscure than to explain the two systems. A number of compendia dating from this later time exist. They are well adapted to serve as introductions not only to the Nyaya-Vaiseshika, but to Indian scientific literature in general. The oldest of these handbooks is the *Sapta-padarthi* of Sivaditya, who cannot have lived later than the twelfth century. A treatise on logic, studied all over India, is the *Bhasa-pariccheda,* a manual of the Navadvipa school, whose author also wrote a commentary on the *Nyaya-sutra* in the year 1634. The best known in Europe of these handbooks is the *Tarka-samgraha* by the south Indian Annam Bhatta. It is a short and clear summary of the most important tenets of logic and dialectic. The date of the author is uncertain, though it cannot be later than the sixteenth century.

Sivaite sects attached themselves closely to the Nyaya and Vaiseshika, though these systems were, as we have seen, purely secular in origin.

The Lokayata System

Outside the orthodox systems was the doctrine of materialism called *lokayata,* 'directed to the world', the founder of which was held to be Charvaka. That it was an old school is indicated by the fact that in the *Vinaya-pitaka* the Buddhist monks were forbidden to occupy themselves with this doctrine. Of the literature of the adherents of Charvaka nothing has survived, and their doctrines are known to us only from the accounts of opponents. We are informed that their philosophy was laid down in a *sutra* attributed to Brihaspati, and in the *Bhaguri* mentioned by Patanjali in the *Mahabhasya.*

It is not surprising that these works have perished, because the materialists were detested by all religious sects, not only as repudiating the Veda, but as hostile to religion in general. They regarded the soul as only an attribute of the body consisting in intelligence. They regarded it as coming into being when the body is formed by the combination of elements, just as the power of intoxication arises from the mixture of certain ingredients. When therefore the body, is destroyed, the soul necessarily disappears. Thus results cannot be produced by transmigration, but by the true nature of things.

Hell, they assert, is nothing but earthly pain produced by earthly causes; and salvation is simply the dissolution of the body. They do not admit the existence of anything supernatural. The Vedas they describe as the incoherent rhapsodies of knaves, and as tainted with the three blemishes of falsehood, self-contradiction, and tautology; Vedic teachers as imposters, whose doctrines are mutually destructive; and the ritual of the Brahmins as of no value except as a means of livelihood.

If an animal that is sacrificed reaches heaven, why, they ask, does the sacri-ficer not rather offer his own father? The only end of man they regard as sensual pleasure to be enjoyed by ignoring as far as possible any pains it may involve. 'While life remains,' they say, 'let a man live happily, let him feed on pleasant food, even though he run into debt; when once the body has been reduced to ashes, how can it ever return to life?'

It is perhaps not surprising that the literature in which such views are set forth should not have survived in an environment so uncongenial to them as the general trend of Indian thought.

•

The question whether Greek and Indian philosophy were in any way connected has often engaged the attention of scholars. **The characteristic peculiarities of Indian philosophical literature are such that the possibility of the Greeks ever having directly studied Indian philosophical texts is extremely remote.** Any influence exercised by Indian on Greek philosophy must have been due to oral intercourse. The similarity between the Eleatic school of Xenophanes and Parmenides and the Vedanta is probably due to parallel development rather than borrowing. The influence of the Sankhya on Greek philosophy is possible and perhaps even probable. In the case of Pythagoras, Indian influence is by some scholars thought to be undoubted. On the other hand, Greek influence on the Nyaya and Vaiseshika has been suggested though not proved. Thus the Aristotelian doctrine of the syllogism may have influenced the later development of Indian logic, and the atomic theory of Empedocles may have affected the parallel atomic doctrine in India.

Legal Literature

Dharma-sastra is the designation of legal literature in Sanskrit. Here the word *dharma* has a much wider connotation than 'law', for it includes religion, custom, good conduct, duty, in fact all that comes within the sphere of right. The oldest treatises on this subject are the *dharma-sutras,* which grew up in close connexion with the works on ritual (*kalpa*). They are not compendia of law, but deal with the religious duties of man. They proceeded from the Vedic schools and were used by Brahmins for the purpose of instruction, not for practical application in law courts. They form part of Vedic literature, giving directions regarding daily religious rites, purifications, penances, duties, and rights of householders, Brahmins, kings, ascetics, forest-hermits, besides discussions on cosmology and eschatology. It is only where the duties of kings are concerned that sections occur on family law, legal procedure, civil and criminal law (*vyavahara*). They are written in the *sutra* style, but in all of them, verses, generally in the *sloka,* often in the *tristubh* metre, are interspersed.

The best preserved of these works is the *Apastambiya-dharma-sutra,* belonging to the school of Apastamba of the Black *Yajurveda* in south India. On grounds of language and subject-matter it can hardly be estimated to date from later than about 400 B.C. A little later, and attached to the school of Hiranyakesin, is a *sutra* which differs but slightly from that of Apastamba. Somewhat older than Apastamba's is the *sutra* of Baudhayana, also representing a south Indian school of the Black *Yajurveda.* But this work has not been well preserved, for some of its sections are certainly later additions to its original form.

Most probably the oldest of this class of treatises is the *Dharma-sastra* of Gautama, which belongs to a school of the *Samaveda.* Though quoted by some of the earliest Dharma-sutras, it seems to contain some interpolations. Later than Gautama is the *Vasistha-dharma-sutra,* which probably belonged to a north Indian school of the *Rigveda.* This, too, contains a good many interpolations. It quotes a *Dharma-sutra* of Manu, which was probably the basis of the famous *Manava-dharma-sastra.* The latter work once quotes the *Vasistha-dharma-sutra,* which probably dates from some centuries before our era. A more extensive legal work than any of those mentioned is the *Vaisnava-dharma-sastra,* also called the *Visnu-smrti.* It is founded on an old Dharma-sutra of the Kaṫhaka school belonging to the Black *Yajurveda.* The Vishnuite redaction, in which form it has come down to us, cannot date from earlier than about 200 A.D., as is proved by the occurrence of the names of the seven days of the week, including the term *jaiva,* for Thursday, which is based on the Greek name *Zevs.'* The passages in which widow-burning is recommended belong to the same time. But the oldest parts of the work must go back to a very early period, for the texts of the Kathaka school, with which the *Visnu-smrti* is connected, are among the oldest remains of Vedic literature.

A very early and extensive Dharma-sutra, which belongs to the Maitrayaniya school of the Black *Yajurveda,* is that of Harita, quoted by both Apastamba and Baudhayana. As is the case both in the *Baudhayana-sutra* and in the *Vasistha-dharma-sutra,* the *sutras* are interspersed with *slokas* and with *tristubh* stanzas.

Although the chronology of the legal literature is uncertain, it can be assumed with probability that the older Dharma-sutras belonging to the Vedic schools date from between 800 and 300 B.C. At any rate, they represent the oldest phase of the legal literature, because they characteristically deal with religious duties and rites to a far greater extent than with secular law. Thus the juristic part of the *Apastamba-dharma-sutra* amounts to only about one-seventeenth of the whole work.

The teaching of *dharma* in Vedic schools early gave place to general law schools meant for all classes. It was in these legal schools that the metrical Dharma-sastras and Smritis arose. These were no longer handbooks for the narrow circle of a particular Vedic school, but for the teaching of the religious and secular rights and duties of all the three twice-born classes. These manuals naturally became more extensive, and treated law in the strict sense in much greater detail. The *sutra* style was no longer adequate for the purpose, and the metrical form, especially the *sloka* verse, long familiar as the vehicle of the simple epic, as well as of the didactic poetry so closely akin to the epic, was adopted. This sententious poetry was indeed one of the chief sources of the Dharma-sastras. The teachers of *dharma* themselves name as its sources, besides *sruti* and *smrti,* the practice of the cultured (*sistah*) and customary law (*acara*). The rules of the latter two authorities were early expressed in *slokas,* many of which go back to the time of the Dharma-sutras or even farther. Much old material is thus preserved in the Dharma-sastras, which are themselves chronologically later productions. Numerous ethical and legal maxims in metre are found in the epics, especially the *Mahabharata.* Hence the epic (*itihasa*) is stated to be a fifth source of *dharma.*

These metrical law-books have been studied as authoritative for centuries all over India down to the present day. Though claiming validity for all castes, they are primarily written in the interests of Brahmins. But they deal to a much larger extent with the rights and duties of the king.

The Smritis

No work has enjoyed so great a reputation and authority throughout India for centuries as the *Manava-dharma-sastra,* also called the *Manu-smriti,* or 'Code of Manu'. Not only in India, but among early European Sanskrit scholars, fantastic views were held regarding the age of this work. Thus Sir William Jones attributed it to the thirteenth century B.C., and A.W. v. Schlegel to not later than 1000 B.C. It has been shown to be based on an antecedent *Dharma-sutra,* which was later versified. It is in fact probably one of the earlier examples of the transformation of an old Dharma-sutra into a metrical Dharma-sastra. Even yet the limits of time within which it must have come into being have not been narrowed down to a shorter period than about four centuries:

between 200 B.C. and 200 A.D.

The relation of the *Manu-smriti* to the *Mahabharata* is of some importance in investigating its date. In the latest sections of the *Mahabharata,* especially Book XIII, passages of a *Dharma-sastra* of Manu are quoted and actually occur in our *Manu-smriti.* On the other hand, a large number of identical verses occur in both works without being designated as quotations. As the varieties of reading are sometimes better in the one text, sometimes in the other, the conclusion is that such verses have in both texts been derived from the floating sententious poetry which we have seen to be one of the sources of the metrical Dharma-sastras, and of which it would be vain to attempt to assign the priority in the one text or the other. We seem to be justified in inferring that the oldest parts of the *Mahabharata* are older than our *Manu-smriti;* that its latest parts quote a work which was virtually identical with our *Manu-smriti*; and that both texts borrowed a considerable amount of identical material from the sententious poetry that was the common property of the educated. No more definite chronological conclusions are justified in the present state of our knowledge.

The contents of the *Manu-smriti* show that the interval between it and the oldest Dharma-sutras, which, like Apastamba's, have remained unmodified by interpolation, must be considerable. The purely legal parts of the *Manu-smriti* amount to rather more than one-fourth of the whole work. Owing to the sources from which a considerable portion of the book is derived, it produces on the whole the impression of a didactic poem, in which imagery, similes, and elevated diction abound. The author evidently aimed at producing a literary work rather than a dry manual of jurisprudence.

A testimony to the widespread fame of *Manu* is the number of commentaries composed on it in every part of India. Medhatithi, who lived in Kashmir, probably in the ninth century, was the author of the oldest surviving commentary; he frequently refers to predecessors, some of whom he speaks of as ancient. Another commentator, probably belonging to the twelfth century, is Govindaraja, whose work is distinguished by accuracy, and is valuable for its explanations of difficult passages. The best known, because most frequently printed, commentary is that of Kulluka, written at Benares in the fifteenth century. It is of little independent value, being virtually a plagiarism of the earlier work of Govindaraja.

The reputation of *Manu* extended to Burma, Siam, and the islands of Java and Bali, whose law has been greatly influenced by this code.

Next in age to *Manu.* is the *Yajnavalkya-smrti,* the Dharma-sastra of Yajnavalkya. It is probably based on a no longer extant *Dharma-sutra* belonging to eastern India and attached to the White *Yajurveda;* for it has been shown to have affinities with the *Grhya-sutra* of that Veda. It is evident that *Yajnavalkya* represents a more advanced stage than *Manu,* for it is more concise, more clearly arranged, and more systematic. While *Manu* confines the sphere of evidence to the statements of witnesses, and in the matter of ordeals treats only of those by fire and water, *Yajnavalkya* deals exhaustively with written documents as evidence, and knows five kinds of ordeals. This law-book also contains far fewer passages resembling didactic poetry than *Manu.* Many indications appear in it that it dates from no earlier than 300 A.D.

The most famous of the many commentaries on *Yajnavalkya* is the *Mitaksara* of Vijnanesvara,. This is, however, more than a commentary, being really a juristic work based on *Yajnavalkya.* The author was a south Indian who lived between 1050 and 1100 A.D. His work early acquired a great reputation in Benares as well as, the Deccan, and as late as the beginning of last century, acquired a new importance within the jurisdiction of British India through Colebrooke's translation (1810) of its section on the law of inheritance. Quite a number of commentaries were written on this authoritative work.

The date of the *Narada-smriti* seems to be somewhat later still, as would appear from internal evidence. It is much more advanced in its treatment of law than *Manu*. Thus it emphasizes written procedure and documentary evidence. It has much more elaborate subdivisions under various heads. Thus *Manu's* eighteen titles of the law have in *Narada* 132 subordinate divisions. The occurrence of the word *dinara* (the Latin *denarius*), as the name of a gold coin, shows that the *Narada-smriti* could not have come into being before the second century B.C., and that it was probably not composed before the fourth century A.D., because though Roman gold coins were already in abundant use in India in the first century A.D., the word *dinara* is not met with till 400 A.D. in inscriptions.

The *Brhaspati-smriti,* of which only fragments have been preserved in medieval quotations, is still more closely connected with *Manu* than *Narada;* for it resembles a commentary, which, always starting from the dicta of *Manu,* supplements and extends them. It deals exhaustively with legal documents, and recommends widow-burning, which is not done in the earlier law-books. Representing, taken in all, a more advanced stage of development than *Narada,* it probably came into existence a century or two later.

There are numerous other Dharma-sastras which also are known only in a fragmentary way from quotations. Many other later Smritis, preserved in manuscripts or printed in collections, deal not with the whole of *dharma,* but only with parts. One of the more important and comparatively old legal works is the *Parasara-smriti,* which was commented on by Madhava in the fourteenth century. It is uncertain whether this Parasara is identical with the one mentioned by Medhatithi in the ninth century.

Of greater importance than the later law-books are the *Dharma-nibandhas,* which are systematic and sometimes very extensive works on *dharma.* This type of legal literature began to be produced from about 1100 A.D., and continues to appear even at the present day (1925). Many of these works are important on account of the numerous quotations they contain from older works that have since been lost. One of the earliest books of this class is the *Smriti-kalpa-taru* by Lakshmidhara, the minister of a king who is identical with Govindachandra of Kanauj (1105-43 A.D.).

Between 1260 and 1309 A.D. Hemadri wrote a bulky work entitled *Caturvarga-cintamani,* which in five chapters deals with vows, almsgiving, places of pilgrimage, salvation, funeral rites (*sraddha*), and the sacrificial calendar. It also teems with quotations from the Puranas and the Smritis. Other compendia treat of law in the strict sense (*vyavahara*). One of these is the *Dharma-ratna* of Jimuta-vahana, written probably in the fifteenth century. A portion of this work, the *Dayabhaga,* on the law of inheritance, is the chief authority of the Bengal school of law, and was translated into English by Colebrooke.

In the eighteenth century several *Dharma-nibandhas* were compiled by pandits who were commissioned for the purpose in the interest of the law-courts.

Science of Practical Life (*Arthasastra*)

In connexion with the doctrine, which we find mentioned before our era, that there are three chief aims in human life (*trivarga*): the good (*dharma*), the useful (*artha*), and the desirable (*kama*), there was developed a branch of literature called *arthasastra,* comprehending practical arts, economics, administration, and especially politics. The latter as an independent branch is also called *nitisastra* or 'science of conduct or government'. Since the king was regarded as requiring a knowledge of the other aspects of *arthasastra,* the term *nitisastra* is sometimes used as a synonym. Because to the Indian mind government meant monarchical rule only, this science is also called *rajaniti,* 'the conduct of kings', that is, the policy of government. The extant metrical Dharma-sastras presuppose *arthasastra* as a special science, and the twelfth book of the *Mahabharata* attests its existence. The former teach duties ultimately based on revelation; the latter the measures that conduce to gaining material results apart from considerations of religion or morality. Thus the poet Magha speaks of self-aggrandisement and the subjugation of the enemy constituting the essence of policy (*niti*). The Buddhists were entirely opposed to its methods, rejecting the notion that morality should give way to advantage, and regarding *niti* as systematic mendacity.

By far the most important work of this type of

literature is the *Kautiliya-arthasastra,* a treatise on the art of government and administration attributed to Kautilya (otherwise Chanakya or Vishnugupta), the minister of Chandragupta of the Maurya dynasty. No work of Indian literature supplies such full information on the political and economic conditions of ancient India. Though its existence was long known, it was not edited till 1906. It is written in prose consisting in a mixture of *sutra* and commentary which it is hardly possible to separate. A few verses are interspersed in it, and every chapter ends with one or more stanzas generally well adapted in sense to the preceding prose. As regards its teaching of duty, the *Arthasastra* is entirely Brahminical, inculcating the duties of each caste and each stage of life exactly like the *smritis.*

One of its chapters is concerned with the various means of getting rid of traitors and enemies of the state; and nothing, it is indicated, is too perfidious to accomplish such an end. Besides the unique extent to which this work throws light on the life of ancient India, it would have a special chronological value if it could be shown to be the work of King Chandragupta's famous minister. For then we should have the first and only certainly datable evidence regarding Indian literature and civilization for such an early period as the fourth century B.C. But unfortunately we know nothing of any activity of Kautilya either as a teacher or an author. Chandragupta ascended the throne about 322 B.C., and in 302 B.C. the Greek Megasthenes came to his court as the ambassador of Seleukos Nikator. We possess a fragmentary account of India written by him during his long stay in the country. But neither he nor any other ancient author knows anything of the celebrated minister of Chandragupta.

A careful comparison of Megasthenes' account with Kautilya's *Arthasastra* does not confirm the assumption that these two authors were contemporaries. No appreciable agreement is to be found between the conditions prevailing at the time of Asoka and those described by Kautilya. Patanjali in the *Mahabhasya* mentions the Mauryas and the court (*sabha*) of Chandragupta, but not a word about Kautilya. All our information about Kautilya belongs to the region of legend and poetry; and even here there is nothing about his activity as a teacher and author. In the *Arthasastra* itself there is no trace of any reference to the Nandas, the Mauryas, or King Chandragupta and the conditions prevailing in his day.

It is true that final verses in the first two chapters and at the conclusion of the whole book state the *Arthasastra* to be the work of Kautilya, but the probability is that the chapters containing these verses were added at the final redaction of the work. In the book itself the author is never called Chanakya or Vishnugupta, but always only Kautilya, and it is highly improbable that the minister of Chandragupta would have called himself by a name signifying 'crookedness', 'perfidy'. The name of Kautilya, too, is mentioned in the same way as in Sutras, to indicate the text of a school, not of an individual author.

The conclusion thus appears to be justified that the *Arthasastra* is ascribed to Kautilya because the legendary minister of Chandragupta was regarded as the typical master of the science of politics, cunning and unscrupulous, but devoted to his prince. In this way all political maxims came to be traced to Chanakya. Surveying the work as a whole, we find that, in addition to politics in the narrow sense, it contains a mass of material, requiring expert knowledge, on subjects like architecture, mining, military science, and so on, all of which no individual man, even in ancient India, could have mastered. The works of specialists must therefore have been incorporated without much alteration. A long literary activity both in the theory of politics as well as in various technical sciences must be presupposed before all such matter could be combined in a single work.

From a consideration of all the branches of literature which it presupposes or shows agreement with, the conclusion seems justified that it is not older than 200 A.D. at the very earliest. It is valuable to have a work supplying evidence for even so remote a period as this. Some scholars, however, have been inclined to assign this book to so mythical a date as at least 500 years earlier. The designation of Kautilya as the Indian Machiavelli is justified in so far as the unscrupulous methods of both apply to a monarchical state only. But Machiavelli bases his methods on the teaching of history, an aspect entirely absent in Kautilya, who founds his methods solely on theory, as to what means are best adapted to safeguarding the ruler, though his theory probably often corresponds to actually prevailing conditions.

A later and somewhat different kind of work is the *Nitisara* of Kamandaki or Kamandaka. Entirely written in verse, it has rather the nature of a didactic poem than of a manual of politics. Like a Kavya it is divided into cantos. In his introductory verses the author eulogizes Vishnugupta as having by the efficacy of his intrigues secured the earth for Chandragupta. Elsewhere he speaks of Kautilya as his *guru,* that is to say, as the master on whom he draws as his chief source. Probably several centuries lie between Kautilya and Kamandaki, the literary evidence regarding whom points to his dating from between 700 and 750 A.D. Though the contents of the *Nitisara* partially coincide with the *Arthasastra,* a considerable portion differs entirely. Hence its author must have used other sources as well.

In the tenth century the Jain author Somadevasuri composed in Kashmir his *Nitivakyamrta,* or 'Nectar of Political Doctrines'. It shows close dependence on the *Arthasastra,* with which it often verbally agrees. It frequently paraphrases the text, and may then actually serve as its commentary. It is, however, a work of a totally different kind; for it is not a practical manual of politics and economics, but rather an educational work intended for the guidance of kings. The author includes in *niti* not only political wisdom, but also moral conduct. Although a Jain, he assumes the outlook of a Brahmin and is a strict adherent of the caste system. It is a prose work written in short, terse sentences, but not at all in the *sutra* style, the language being clear and simple. The author is fond of introducing sentences of a proverbial type. Such are: 'A man who has not studied science is blind even though possessed of eyes'; 'Better is a world without a king, than having a dunce for a king'. A Jain touch appears in the precept: 'One should not indulge in any sport that involves injury to living beings'.

A short work by the well-known Jaina monk Hemachandra is the *Laghu-arhan-nitisastra*, 'Brief Manual on Politics for Jainas'. It is composed in *slokas* interspersed with occasional explanations in prose. By far the greater part of the work, however, deals not, as its name seems to imply, with politics, but with civil and criminal law in connexion with the Dharma-sastras, especially the *Manu-smriti.*

There are several other works on *niti,* some of them attributed by their writers to mythical sages of old. The editor of two of these endeavoured to show that the ancient Indians were acquainted with fire-arms and gunpowder!

Other Arts

Belonging to the sphere of *arthasastra* are all kinds of manuals dealing with special branches of practical knowledge, such as the **treatment of horses and elephants,** the **art of war** (*dhanurveda*), **architecture,** the **science of gems,** and so on. The term *silpa-sastra,* though strictly speaking the lore of plastic art, is specially applied to architecture, which is also called *vastuvidya*, **'science of building'.** One of the chief works on architecture is the *Mana-sara, or* 'Quintessence of Measurements' as connected with the foundations and building of houses and temples, town-planning, construction of images, and so forth.

There are also works on the **art of music** (*samgita-sastra*) both **vocal** and **instrumental.** At a later stage were produced special handbooks covering the whole ground of musical art: notation, scales, melodies, singing; musical instruments, dance and mimicry; organization of musical bands and of concerts, besides many other details. An old work of the kind is the *Samgita-ratnakara* by Sarangadeva of Kashmir. Nothing more is known about its date than that its commentator Kallinatha lived about 1450 A,D. A later work is the *Samgita-darpana* of Damodara, who not only used the *Samgita-ratnakara,* but took over parts of it word for word; when he differs from his predecessor he probably borrowed from older sources and is to this extent important. There are also monographs on melodies, as the *Raga-vibodha* of Somanatha written in 1609 A.D.

An old science is that of gems, with which Varahamihira shows familiarity in his *Brihat-samhita.* Several works on this subject are extant, but their date is unknown.

Even the **art of thieving** is mentioned in the *Mahabharata* and in one of the early dramas as the subject of a treatise, and one such work has actually been preserved. It is entitled *Sanmukha-kalpa,* or 'Rules of the Six-headed One', that is, of the god of war, Kartikeya, who is regarded as the guardian deity of thieves. **Magic** is an art in which the chief of a robber gang is required to be well-versed.

This subject is sufficiently dealt with by Winternitz in his *Geschichte,* iii. 508-35.

Kamasastra

The literature which is connected with *kama,* the third object of life, and which goes under the designation of *Kamasastra,* or 'Doctrine of Love', cannot be altogether passed over here. The oldest work on the subject is the *Kamasutra* of Mallanaga Vatsyayana, whose treatise is evidently modelled on Kautilya's *Arthasastra,* and who analogously to his prototype may be called the Machiavelli of erotics. The contents of this work appear to us for the most part indecent, but it must be borne in mind that the Indian is always much more outspoken on sexual matters than we are. Like other Sanskrit manuals, it contains many pedantic divisions, classifications, and definitions. It cannot in any way be compared with the 'Arsamatoria' of Ovid. The greater part of the work should be of interest to the ethnologist only but its age alone gives it some importance in the history of literature and civilization. The third section contains some valuable supplementary information on the marriage customs, described in the Grhya- and Dharma-sutras, and the sixth section, which deals with the position of courtesans, is of the greatest interest for the history of civilization.

Though this is the earliest extant work on the subject, Vatsyayana himself mentions that he had many predecessors. The *Kamasastra* has a close connexion with the writers of Kavya, for its study is enjoined on these poets, and the manuals of poetics (*alamkara*) contain many sections that touch upon the subjects contained in the *Kamasastra.* Both Subandhu and Bhavabhuti are thoroughly familiar with the *Kamasutra,* the latter even quoting it. This shows that Vatsyayana's work must have been written before 600 A.D. On the other hand, it is undoubtedly later than Kautilya's *Arthasastra.* We may therefore conjecture that it dates from somewhere about 450 A.D.

There is a very detailed commentary on the *Kamasutra* entitled *Jayamangala* written by Yasodhara Indrapada, who lived in the thirteenth century. A rather extensive literature on erotics nourished in the later period. Of this may be mentioned the *Rati-rahasya,* or 'Secret of Love', composed before 1200 A.D., by Kokkoka, who professes to have used as his sources not only Vatsyayana's teachings, but also those of other exponents of the subject. Another well-known work is the *Ananga-ranga,* 'The Stage of Cupid', by a royal author named Kalyanamalla, who probably lived in the sixteenth century.

Winternitz, *Geschidite,* iii. 536-41, gives a brief account of this subject, together with its bibliography.

Medicine

The beginnings of medical science reach far back into Vedic times. In the magical hymns of the *Atharvaveda* and the magical ceremonies of the ritual literature, especially the *Kausika Sutra,* belonging to this Veda, we find early acquaintance with the healing art and healing plants. Here as elsewhere the magical physician is the first 'medicine man'. This connexion with magic has never been forgotten in India; for even in scientific medical works demons are recognized as originators of disease, and incantations as remedies. In Vedic texts can be traced the beginnings of anatomy, embryology, and hygiene. Thus the *Atharvaveda* and the *Satapatha Brahmana* contain an exact enumeration of the bones of the human skeleton. The old name of medical science is *Ayurveda,* or 'Veda ot Longevity', regarded as one of the supplements of the *Atharvaveda.* The *Ayurveda* according to tradition consisted of eight parts, among which were included demonology (the doctrine of diseases caused by demons) and toxicology (the science of poisons).

The age of medical science in India is attested by its frequent mention in ancient Buddhist literature. In later times, too, the Buddhists showed a partiality for the study of medicine. This is indicated by the detailed account given by the Chinese traveller I-tsing (seventh century A.D.) of the medical science of the Indians. The oldest approximately datable medical texts were also Buddhist. An ancient Sanskrit manuscript containing seven texts was found in 1890 at Kucha in Chinese Turkistan buried in a Buddhist relic-mound (*stupa*). The palaeographical evidence indicates that it dates from about 350 A.D. Three of the seven texts are medical. One of them deals with garlic, which is said to heal many diseases and to prolong life to one hundred years. Another, entitled *Navanitaka* ('Cream'), is an abstract of the best of earlier treatises. The contents include prescriptions of an archaic type, and many medical authorities are mentioned, but none is now known except Susruta. All these manuscripts, which are fragmentary, are in verse, partly even in artificial metres. The language in which they are written is Sanskrit mixed with Prakritisms.

The three ancient authorities on Indian medicine are Charaka, Susruta, and Vagbhata. These names are represented by three Samhitas, that is, large collections or compendia of medicine which were probably based on older special treatises, no longer extant, of different branches of medicine.

The *Charaka-samhita* is, according to its own statement, an adaptation of an older work by an authority named Agnivesa. The Chinese translation (473 A.D.) of the Pali *Tipitaka* states that Charaka was the court physician of King Kanishka. If this statement is correct, Charaka lived in the second century A.D., but the evidence is uncertain. It is, however, clear that the text has not come down to us in its original form. Both the manuscripts and the editions show very divergent readings. Moreover, a Kashmirian named Dridhabala, who lived about 800 A.D., supplied about one-third of the text, besides revising and adding to the whole work. But the original part of the book, which, like the *Kautiliya-arthasastra,* is written in prose, with verse at the end of each chapter, is undoubtedly old, being probably the earliest of the surviving treatises on medicine.

The *Charaka-samhita* consists of eight parts covering the whole field of medical science. One of its statements is that the three mainstays of bodily health are eating, sleep, and abstemiousness. Charaka is a moralist and philosopher as well as a physician. In connexion with hygienic rules and with the doctrine that sin is one of the causes of disease, he also gives many religious and moral precepts. In his discussions about the soul he shows himself familiar with the Sankhya philosophy, as well as with the theory of the syllogism in the Nyaya, and with the categories of the Vaiseshika system.

The oldest commentary on Charaka is that of Chakrapani Datta, which dates from the eleventh century. Long before that time Charaka had been translated into Persian, and thence into Arabic about 800 A.D.

The best known Indian treatise on medicine is the *Susruta-samhita,* which is composed in prose intermixed with verse; but, both in language and matter, it appears to be later than the original part of Charaka's work. The name of Susruta was known in the ninth and tenth centuries to the people of Cambodia in Farther India, as well as to the Arabs, as that of a famous physician. Though it cannot be doubted that Susruta belongs to one of the early centuries of our era and cannot be much later than Charaka, the authenticity of the text of his work in its extant form is guaranteed by the safeguard of commentaries only from the eleventh century onwards. Before that time it was probably subjected to considerable changes. Thus it is said to have undergone a revision at the hands of Nagarjuna. Susruta, as contrasted with Charaka, was particularly partial to surgery, which is hardly touched upon by the earlier author. Susruta requires a high moral standard in the votaries of medical science. Thus he says among other things that priests, friends, neighbours, widows, the poor, and travellers should be treated gratis by the physician as if they were his relations, while to hunters, fowlers, outcasts, and sinners no medical aid at all should be extended.

The oldest commentaries on Susruta no longer survive; the earliest one extant is the *Bhanumati* of Chakrapani Datta, the commentator of the eleventh century already mentioned.

With the name of Vagbhata, the last of the medical trio, are associated two famous works, the *Astanga-samgraha,* 'Compendium of the Eight Branches', and the *Astanga-hrdaya-samhita*, 'Collection of the Quintessence of the Eight Branches' of medicine. Even in form, as being composed in a mixture of prose and verse, the former is older than the latter, which is entirely metrical. The difference between the two works is apparent in their matter also. When quoted by later medical writers the former appears as Vriddha-Vagbhata, the 'old Vagbhata', while the latter is simply called Vagbhata. On these grounds we are justified in assuming that there were really two writers of the name, and that the elder probably lived about 600 A.D., the younger some two centuries later. The elder was probably the man of whom, without mentioning his name, the Chinese traveller I-tsing says that he had recently written a compendium of the eight parts of medical science. The elder was undoubtedly a Buddhist, and probably the younger also. Both of them quote Susruta as well as Charaka.

Much about the same time as the younger Vagbhata, that is, *c.* 800 A.D., was written the *Rog-viniscaya,* 'Investigation of Diseases', by Madhavakara, the son of Indukara. This work is generally called *Madhava-nidana,* or is referred to by the still shorter title of *Nidana.* This is, indeed, the chief Indian work on pathology, in which the most important diseases are treated in detail, and which has remained an authority to all later treatises on the subject. Its celebrity is attested by the number of commentaries to which it gave rise. It is presupposed by Vrinda's *Siddhi-yoga* or *Vrinda-madhava,* which gives prescriptions for all diseases ranging from fever to the results of poisoning. The two works are so intimately connected that they have even been supposed to be by the same author. Chakrapani Datta, a native of Bengal, already mentioned as a commentator on Charaka and Susruta, was also an independent medical author. He wrote in 1060 A.D. the *Chikitsa-sara-samgraha,* a large compendium of therapeutics, based chiefly on the *Siddhiyoga.*

Another medical work is the *Sarngadhara-samhita,* which cannot have been written later than 1200 A.D., as there is a commentary on it by Vopadeva dating from about 1300 A.D. Preparations of opium and quicksilver are mentioned in it as remedies, and the feeling of the pulse in diagnosis is exactly described, subjects which do not occur in earlier treatises. Many other medical works, including monographs, have been written in later centuries, down to quite modern times, but these it would be superfluous to mention here.

There is a very extensive literature that deals with the miraculous healing powers of metallic preparations (called *rasa*) and that belongs to the lower branch of medicine concerned with magic and alchemy. The most important substance here used is quicksilver, which is recommended as an elixir of life, a means of rejuvenation, and a remedy for all kinds of diseases. As quicksilver was also regarded as a means of transmuting baser metals into gold, works dealing with *rasa* belong to the sphere of alchemy also. Such works were already (*c.* 1030 A.D.) known to Alberuni, who speaks of them with great contempt.

Medico-botanical glossaries called *nighantu* were probably known even in ancient times; but the extant dictionaries of this kind are not very old. A Bengal physician named Suresvara or Surapala composed in the year 1075 A.D. a vocabulary of medical botany entitled *Sabda-pradipa.* All these medical glossaries are written in verse.

Even in the nineteenth century a number of works on the remedial substances used in the practice of medicine were composed in Sanskrit.

Though there can be no doubt as to the indigenous origin of Indian medicine, it has many resemblances to the Greek science, some of which can hardly be explained except by the influence of the latter. Several remedies, such as opium and quicksilver, and in diagnosis the feeling of the pulse, Indian medicine owes to the Persians and Arabs. On the other hand, Indian works on medicine (Charaka and Susruta) were translated into Persian and Arabic about 800 A.D. In the Middle Ages Arabic medicine became the chief authority of European physicians and remained so down to the seventeenth century. In this way Indian medical writers became known in Europe, Charaka being repeatedly mentioned in the Latin translations of leading Arab medical writers. In modern times European surgery has borrowed the operation of rhinoplasty, or the surgical formation of artificial noses, from India, where Englishmen became acquainted with the art in the eighteenth century.

The medicine of Tibet, Ceylon, and Farther India is altogether dependent on that of India.

Astronomy

The science of astronomy has almost invariably been associated in India with astrology, its unscientific branch. The same writers are, indeed, often the authors of works on both astronomy and astrology.

The beginnings of Indian astronomy are to be traced in the mythological and cosmological fancies of the Vedic hymns and the Brahmanas. The celestial phenomena of light as subject to an invariable natural law (*rta*) are constantly dwelt on by the Vedic bards. Occasionally we find traces of a more scientific conception of the movements of the heavenly bodies. Thus **one of the Brahmanas observes that the sun does not really rise or set, but produces day and night on the earth by revolving.** The Vedic sacrificers had to make careful chronological calculations with regard to their ritual, having for this purpose to observe accurately the phases of the moon, the course of the sun, the seasons, and especially the zodiac with its twenty-seven or twenty-eight constellations (*naksatras*). The origin of this zodiac, which is also found among the Arabs and the Chinese, is still an open question. The attempts to constitute a calendar for sacrificial and ritual purposes reach far back into Vedic times, but actual works on astronomy do not exist in Vedic literature.

Of the supplementary literature attached to the Vedas under the general name of *Vedangas* only one short work survives from among probably many that dealt with astronomy. It is the *Jyotisa-vedanga,* a brief treatise composed in *slokas* (forty-three in the recension of the *Yajurveda* and thirty-six in that of the *Rigveda*), and concerned exclusively with chronological calculation. Only partially intelligible on account both of its *sutra*-like style and of the corrupt state of the text, it chiefly describes the five-year *yuga,* or cycle of five years of 366 days, as well as the positions of moon and sun at the solstices and at new- and full-moon in the circle of the *naksatras,* or lunar mansions.

To the earlier post-Vedic period of Indian astronomy belong the following works: the *Vrddha-garga-samhita,* which, however, is chiefly astrological; an extensive astronomical *Upanga* of the Jains, the *Suriya-pannati,* or 'Instructions regarding the Sun'; also some supplementary treatises of the *Atharvaveda,* which are mostly astronomical. There is also an astronomical fragment preserved among the Weber MSS. which were purchased at Leh in Ladakh by the missionary F. Weber. Two other works are known from quotations only. The astronomical-cosmological sections of the *Mahabharata,* the Puranas, and tlie *Manava-dharmasastra* belong to the same age: none of these works show any trace of the influence of Greek astronomy. Here we first come across the doctrine of the four ages called *krta, treta, dvapara,* and *kali,* of which each preceding one surpasses in excellence that which follows.

The later post-Vedic period of Indian astronomy is entirely post-Christian. As opposed to the pre-Christian stage, it is scientific in character as well as no longer purely Indian. The system of astronomy here developed, in fact, presupposes knowledge of Greek astronomy. The works belonging to this period may be divided into four classes: 1. *Siddhantas* or handbooks giving a detailed account of a complete system of astronomy; 2. *Karanas* or works serving as guides for rapid and convenient astronomical calculations; 3. Works with astronomical tables facilitating calculations; and 4. Numerous commentaries on older works often containing valuable quotations from treatises that have been lost.

The oldest and most important complete extant work of this period is the *Surya-siddhanta,* which, composed in *slokas,* is divided into four chapters. The present form of the text is not the original one; but its chief teachings are those of Greek astronomy. There seems even to be an allusion to a foreign source in the introductory verses, where the book is stated to have been revealed in the city of Romaka, which must refer to Rome or Alexandria. The peculiarly Indian impression made by this work is due to the enormous duration of the cosmic ages that it lays down, to conceptions such as that of Mount Meru being situated at the North Pole, by the acceptance of the traditional views as to the conjunctions of the planets with the lunar mansions, and other features. The aim of the author was in fact to retain as many of the old views as was compatible with the new doctrines and to adapt the latter as far as possible to the earlier methods and calculations.

The *Surya-siddhanta* is one of the five old Siddhantas described by the famous astronomer and astrologer Varahamihira in his *Panca-siddhantika,* which gives the doctrines of the five Siddhantas that were authoritative in his time in the form of a Karana. Internal evidence shows that this work was composed in the year 505 A.D. The account that Varahamihira here gives of the four Siddhantas other than the *Surya-siddhanta* is all the more important as these four (the *Pitamaha-,* the *Vasistha-,* the *Paulisa;* and the *Romaka-siddhanta*) are no longer extant. Judged by the evidence of the *Panca-siddhantika,* the clearest traces of Greek influence appear to have been found in the *Romaka-siddhanta.* The length of the year was here calculated in exactly the same way as it was by Hipparchos (second century B.C.), and after him by Ptolemy (second century A.D.). The author also took a *yuga,* of cosmic age, to consist of 2,850 solar years, thus departing entirely from the Indian tradition of the duration of such an age.

Different from the old *Romaka-siddhanta* is the work with the same title that was revised and alleged to have been improved by Srishena after Varahamihira. Of this work Brahmagupta says it had borrowed so much from Lata, Aryabhata, and others that it had the appearance of a much-patched garment. But though the doctrines of the older *Romaka-siddhanta* are Greek, it nevertheless diverges in essential points from Greek astronomy. It further differs quite considerably from the *Surya-siddhanta,* which also shows Greek influence. These two Siddhantas must therefore go back to different sources. But since the *Surya-siddhanta,* though agreeing generally with the astronomy of Ptolemy (140 A.D.), yet also differs from him, it is impossible to answer with certainty the question when and through what works Greek astronomy influenced that of India. The uncertainty is all the greater since we know no more of the date of the five Siddhantas than that they were regarded by Varahamihira about 500 A.D. as authoritative works. All therefore we can say is that they must have come into existence in the early centuries after Christ, perhaps in the fourth.

Among some older astronomers mentioned by Varahamihira is Aryabhata, whose work, the *Aryabhatiya,* is of equal importance in the history of mathematics and of astronomy. Written in the *arya* metre, it consists of four parts. The first of these deals with a system of numeral notation peculiar to Aryabhata and with the fundamental elements of the system; the second gives a brief summary of his mathematical teachings; the third contains the outlines of astronomical calculations of time; while the fourth is concerned with the celestial sphere. Aryabhata was probably the first who concisely summarized the system developed in the Siddhanta, without, however, introducing many improvements. His point of view is much the same as that of the author of the *Surya-siddhanta.* There is, however, **one point in which he showed great originality: he maintained the daily rotation of the earth round its axis,** explaining the daily rotation of the celestial sphere as only apparent. It cannot be proved that this doctrine, which was rejected by the later Indian astronomers, was adopted by him from the Greeks. Both Varahamihira and Brahmagupta assailed this doctrine, just as the Greek doctrine was long combated in Europe. Aryabhata was, according to his own statement, born in 476 A.D. and wrote his work in 499 A.D.

An extensive astronomical work entitled *Arya-siddhanta,* by another but later Aryabhata, was known to Bhaskara and has been preserved.

The most famous of the Indian astronomers who lived after Varahamihira were Brahmagupta and Bhaskaracharya. The former, according to his own statement, wrote his *Brahmasphuta-siddhanta* in the year 628 A.D. He generally agrees with his predecessors, but his treatment of his subject-matter is more detailed and methodical. The eleventh chapter of his work is exclusively concerned with criticizing his predecessors, especially Aryabhata. Though Brahmagupta is chiefly eminent as a mathematician, some of his chapters are devoted to the solution of astronomical problems.

The last famous astronomer, Bhaskaracharya, was born in 1114 A.D. and produced the *Siddhanta-siromani,* written in the *arya* metre in 1150 A.D. He enjoys a great reputation, especially as a mathematician, and in astronomy his work is regarded as second only to the *Surya-siddhanta.* But the high value attached to his work is due solely to the fact that it represents the old system more completely and clearly than earlier works do, and that Bhaskara himself has added a commentary in which the usually concise rules are explained and proved in detail. But Bhaskara teaches nothing new, and is in fact completely dependent on Brahmagupta. His work consists of four parts, of which the first two, entitled *Lilavati* and *Bijaganita,* form the mathematical introduction, while the other two, the *Graha-ganitadhyaya* and the *Goladhyaya,* deal with astronomy proper.

A second work by Bhaskara, the *Karana-kutuhala,* was written in 1178.

From the centuries between Brahmagupta and Bhaskara few astronomical books are known.

With the conquest of India by the Muhammedans the Perso-Arabic influence on Indian astronomy began, but it was not strong enough to oust the old indigenous science. In later centuries the last work of any importance on Indian astronomy was the *Siddhanta-tattva-viveka* of Kamalakara, written in 1658 A.D. Though borrowing from Perso-Arabic astronomy, it is essentially based on the *Surya-siddhanta* and attacks Bhaskara. The old Indian astronomical works have never altogether lost their authority, even since European science has become known.

Astrology

Astrology, or the theory of the influence of the stars on human life, has been very intimately connected with astronomy in India. The belief in the importance of celestial phenomena as good or bad omens, and in the possibility of inferring the fortunes of men and of prognosticating future events from the position of the heavenly bodies, is extremely old in India as well as in other eastern countries with an ancient civilization. Even in the Brahmanas we hear of stars that were 'favourable' or 'unfavourable' at weddings and other ceremonies. According to the Dharmasutras, an astrologer is as indispensable to the king as the *purohita* (or domestic chaplain). On the other hand, occupation with astrology, as with magic, is regarded as causing impurity. Buddhist monks, too, were forbidden to have anything to do with astrology, soothsaying, and similar superstitions.

The older works on astrology have been almost entirely lost, having been ousted by Varahamihira, who attained the highest authority as a teacher of the subject. The only one of the earlier treatises that has come down to us is the *Vrddha-garga-samhita;* but it is very doubtful if even that work has been preserved in an approximately original form. It is interesting to note that here is to be found a verse in which the dependence of India on Greek astronomy is acknowledged: 'The Greeks indeed are barbarous, but this science is well established among them; therefore even they are honoured like seers, how much more a Brahmin who is an astrologer.'

According to Varahamihira, the *jyotih-sastra,* or 'Science of Stars', which embraces astronomy and astrology, is divided into three branches: *tantra,* which deals with calculating astronomy; *hora,* which is concerned with the horoscope; and *sakha* or *samhita,* which teaches natural astrology, that is to say, the doctrine of omens derivable from occurrences in nature generally, but especially from celestial phenomena.

The chief work of Varahamihira, who dealt with all departments of astrology, is the *Brihat-samhita,* which is at the same time the most important work on natural astrology. It may even be called one of the most important works of Indian literature in general. For as natural astrology is concerned with all departments of existence, the most diverse aspects of public and private life come to be touched upon in this work, which thus assumes quite an encyclopaedic character. It is of great importance even for the history of religion, in which respect it has not been exploited nearly sufficiently. This astrological work is of appreciable value even as a specimen of artificial poetry, for many passages rise to a considerable level of poetical merit. Thus the author writes: 'As a night without a lamp, as a sky without the sun, so is a king without astrologers: like a blind man he wanders on his path.'

Great importance being attached to the teachings of astrology in the building of a new house, the digging of wells, the laying out of gardens and tanks, the search for underground water, the construction of idols, many chapters deal with these subjects. Some are concerned with jewels, while others have affinity with the *Kamasastra.* Eleven chapters again form a treatise called 'augury' (*sakuna*). Although two chapters of the *Brihat-samhita* are concerned with weddings, Varahamihira also wrote a separate astrological treatise on the auspicious times for marriage. He further wrote another work dealing with the omens on the occasion of a king's marching out to war and entitled *Yoga-yatra,* 'Expedition at Lucky Conjunctions of Stars'.

While that part of the *Jyotih-sastra* which is concerned with natural astrology is chiefly a genuine product of Indian pseudo-science, its aspect dealing with the horoscope, and called by the Sanskrit term *jataka,* 'nativity', or the Greek name *hora,* is entirely under the influence of Greek astronomy. The contents of these horoscopic works, which also contain Greek technical terms, correspond entirely to the Greek books dealing with this subject.

Varahamihira also devoted to this branch of astronomy a large work entitled *Brhaj-jataka,* also called *Hora-sastra,* and a shorter one, the *Laghu-jataka,* the former of which is the best known and most studied. These works are concerned with foretelling the fortunes of a human being from the positions of heavenly bodies at the time of his birth.

This 'science' probably had its origin among the Babylonians, from whom it was conveyed by the Greeks to other peoples. It is, however, not quite certain when it reached the Indians from the Greeks: the evidence seems on the whole to point to the third century A.D. About 600 A.D., Prithuyasas, the son of Varahamihira, wrote an astrological work entitled *Hora-satpancasika.* The commentaries of Bhattotpala, dating from the tenth century, on this and on all the works of Varahamihira, are important because of the numerous quotations from older works that they contain. He is also himself the author of a *Hora-sastra* in seventy-five verses.

As regards the extremely extensive astrological literature of later times, mention need only be made of the *Jyotirvid-abharana,* 'The Ornament of Astrologers', probably written in the sixteenth century. In this work, the author of which calls himself Kalidasa, occurs the celebrated verse about the 'nine gems' at the court of King Vikramaditya, on which the theory of contemporaneousness of various authors and the date of Kalidasa was at one time based. But the value of this evidence is practically none, because this work is late, as it refers to Arabic astrology and is not mentioned till 1661, when it is quoted in a commentary.

After Varahamihira's time a special type of astrological works came into being under the name of *Muhurta* (primarily meaning an hour of forty-eight minutes), the object of which is to fix the moment of time (*muhurta*) favourable not only for religious ceremonies, family festivals, such as weddings, but also for journeys and other undertakings of daily life.

After the beginning of the Arabic conquest, the influence of Perso-Arabian astrology resulted in the rise of a special class of works called Tajik (from the Persian word for 'Arabic'), which are derived from Arabic sources.

Works on omens and portents, soothsaying, interpretation of dreams, and so forth are infinitely numerous. The only one that need be mentioned here is the *Svapna-cintamani,* 'Thought-gem on Dreams', which is of interest both for religious and for literary history. It is a handbook for the interpretation of dreams, by Jagaddeva, who in writing it made, as he himself states, much use of medical literature. The dreams mentioned by him often show a striking agreement with fairy-tale motives.

Mathematics

Mathematical science, as well as astrology, was in India pursued in the closest connexion with astronomy. Thus arithmetic and algebra form parts of the astronomical works of Aryabhata, Brahmagupta, and Bhaskara. The theory that our decimal system is derived from India still holds the field, though the objections raised against this view appear to require a new examination of the question.

The most important mathematical texts are the first two sections of the *Aryabhatiya,* tlie *Ganit-adhyaya* and the *Kuttak-adhyaya* in the *Brahma-sphuta-siddhanta* of Brahmagupta, and the *Lilavati* on arithmetic, and the *Bijaganita* on algebra in the *Siddhanta-siromani* of Bhaskara. The latter remarks at the end of his section on algebra that he had compiled his work from the too diffuse treatises of Brahmagupta and others. In the works of Brahmagupta and of Bhaskara we have the mathematical achievements of the Indians in their most highly developed form. Simple arithmetic is here described as concerned with the 'eight operations' consisting in addition, subtraction, multiplication, division, raising to the square and the cube, and the extraction of the square and the cube root. The methods employed are on the whole similar to our own. Then follow rules about fractions, about the zero, and about the practical applications of arithmetic, comprising the rule of three, the calculation of interest, and so on.

Algebra was also highly developed. Both Brahmagupta and Bhaskara handle a number of simple equations. The following is a sum involving such an equation from Bhaskara's *Lilavati.* 'Of a swarm of bees one-fifth settled on a Kadamba flower and one-third on a Silindra blossom;

one bee remained over, hovering in the air, attracted at the same time by the charming perfume of a jasmine and of a pandanus. Tell me, charming one, the number of the bees.' **These treatises also solve equations with more than one unknown quantity, as well as equations of a higher degree. In all these respects Indian algebra rises appreciably above the level attained by Diophantus, the Greek algebraist of Alexandria (c. 250 A.D.).** The Indian mathematicians had by this time arrived at very advanced results in analysis, and, what represents the highest level of their attainments in the mathematical field, they had discovered a method of solving indeterminate equations of the second degree. This method is by a high mathematical authority (Hankel) declared to be the most delicate operation in the theory of numbers that had been achieved before the time of the great French astronomer Lagrange (eighteenth century).

The beginnings of geometry go back to a period of high antiquity in India, for a considerable amount of geometrical knowledge is to be found in the *Sulva-sutras,* or 'String Rules', which form a part of the general Vedic ritual (*kalpa*) *sutra* works. These give the rules for the laying out of the sacrificial ground, for the construction of the fire-altars, and other arrangements necessary for the performance of the single great sacrifices. The design of the sacrificial ground with its most important constituent parts made the construction of right angles, squares, and circles, as well as the transformation of plane figures into others of equal area, a matter of necessity. To sacrificial experts it was of the utmost moment that the measurement of the sacrificial ground by means of cords (*sulva*) stretched between stakes should be carried out accurately according to rule. These practical requirements resulted in a considerable aggregate of geometrical knowledge, including the Pythagorean proposition (worked out in Euclid I. 47). Thus the ritual experts understood how to transform rectangles into squares, squares into circles, as well as vice versa. It is probable that such geometrical knowledge based on practical operations goes back even to the time of the Vedic hymns.

The geometrical attainments of the Indians in later times, however, fell far short of those of the Greeks. Though there are agreements between the former and the Greek mathematician Heron (third century B.C.), it is probable that they acquired independently the geometrical knowledge found in the *Sulva-sutras*. In the eighteenth century a Sanskrit translation of the elements of Euclid was made from the Arabic by a writer named Samrad Jagannatha.

Trigonometry was known to the Indians in its application to astronomical calculations, and it is to be assumed that they obtained their knowledge of it from the Greeks in connexion with astronomy.

❐ ❐